# HOME
# MUSIC PRODUCTION

## Getting Started

Stephan Earl

# Home Music Production

# Getting Started

by
Stephan Earl

Published by
SearlStudio Publishing
www.searlstudio.com

ISBN: 978-0-9883670-0-5 (ebook)
ISBN 978-0-9883670-1-2 (print)

# Acknowledgments

I want to thank my family and especially my loving wife Katie for her support, and for putting up with my extensive passion for music and music production gear.

### Copy Editor

Megan Peterson Morrow

### Front Cover Design & Illustrations

Stephan Earl

# Contents

INTRODUCTION ...............................................................7

    About This Book .......................................................9
    Who is This Book for? ...............................................9
    What Will You Learn? ..............................................10

CHAPTER 1: UNDERSTANDING THE BASICS .................11

    Terminology ..........................................................11
    Tools You Will Need ................................................15

CHAPTER 2: CHOOSING THE RIGHT COMPUTER.........17

    PC vs. Mac..............................................................17
    Laptop vs. Desktop ................................................18
    RAM ......................................................................20
    CPU .......................................................................21
    Disk Drives .............................................................22

CHAPTER 3: EXTERNAL AUDIO AND MIDI HARDWARE 27

    Audio Interfaces.....................................................27
    MIDI Controllers .....................................................35
    Using an iPad as a Controller ................................41
    Microphones.........................................................43
    Reference Monitors ...............................................54
    Cabling .................................................................56

## CHAPTER 4: DIGITAL AUDIO WORKSTATION (DAW) ... 63

What is a DAW? ............................................................. 63
Which DAW is Right for You? ...................................... 63

## CHAPTER 5: VIRTUAL INSTRUMENTS AND EFFECTS ....... 69

DAW Plug-in Formats.................................................... 69
Jack of All Trades vs. Master of One ......................... 71
Virtual Instruments....................................................... 74
Virtual Effects............................................................... 82

## CHAPTER 6: GOING MOBILE ......................................... 91

Using an iPad for Music Production............................ 91
Mobile DAW Apps ........................................................ 92
Synthesizer and Groove Apps..................................... 93
Connecting an iPad to Your Studio ........................... 95

## CHAPTER 7: SETTING UP YOUR STUDIO ...................... 101

Room Setup and Acoustics......................................... 101
Working Ergonomically ............................................... 108
Home Studio Setup Examples ..................................... 110
Safeguarding Your Home Studio ................................ 116

## CHAPTER 8: FINAL THOUGHTS ................................... 119

# INTRODUCTION

## About the Author

I discovered music in 1981 when I entered the fifth grade and was introduced to the clarinet. I enjoyed playing the instrument, and became even more captivated with music a year later at Christmas when my aunt gave me a Casio keyboard. It was called the VL-Tone VL-1 and had tiny buttons in place of keys. I loved to play the little pre-recorded tunes it came with, but even more, I loved to create my own melodies. Suddenly, the composer in me was born.

At my home recording studio in 1992.

Over the next few years, I upgraded to bigger Casio keyboards that eventually included the ability to record melodies. This was my introduction to sequencing music, and it allowed me to compose musical ideas, then compose and play new parts on top of them. While this may sound primitive by today's standards, this was state-of-the-art to me while on a pre-teen budget back in the early '80s.

In 1985, I was accepted into the prestigious Fiorello H. Laguardia High School for Music and the Performing Arts in New York City as a tenor saxophone player. By that time I was playing a few woodwind instruments, including flute, clarinet and tenor saxophone, and had built up my home recording studio to include a Roland JX-3P, Casio CZ-101, Alesis HR-16 drum machine and an Alesis MMT-8 hardware sequencer, which all went into a Tascam 4-track tape recorder.

I was introduced to computer-based recording in 1988 when my school started an electronic music composition program, where they used PC-based software called Sequencer Plus by Voyetra. Almost immediately, I saw the benefits of computer-based sequencing. I began producing music for local artists and earned enough money to purchase a computer and a copy of Sequencer Plus. I've been using a computer to record music ever since.

For several years after high school, I composed and produced music for many local performing artists in the New York City area before deciding to take a break from music composing and production.

When I returned to music production in 2005, computer-based production technology had advanced from the days of being a purely MIDI sequencing tool to being the complete digital audio workstations we have today. Also, with the advancement in computer CPU power, the need for external hardware effects processors, samplers and synthesizers had diminished. I quickly found myself being overwhelmed by a sea of music production tools, with no idea where to start. At that time, there seemed to be very few resources available to help me ascertain what the best products were, and where I should invest my limited resources.

After a few years of trial and error with purchasing equipment and selling many items on eBay, I decided start a blog to help other musicians in my shoes. And this is how www.HomeMusicProduction.com got started.

## About This Book

I originally began this project as a blog, www.HomeMusicProduction.com. I wanted to share my experiences with other home recording musicians who were either looking for information to improve their existing home recording setups, or were building a music production workstation from scratch.

During the course of two years, I received emails and comments from music production enthusiasts, hobbyists and semi-professionals who were looking for more in-depth information on many topics. These topics ranged from, "what is the best way to design a music production workstation?" to "what computer is the best for music production?" to "which virtual instruments are the best for a particular purpose?" As I began to research certain topics in bookstores and online, I realized there weren't many comprehensive resources that addressed all these questions from start to finish. So I decided to assemble these answers into one comprehensive source of information that could be used as a starting guide, and could also be used for further reference as your music production knowledge increases.

❖ Music production technology is ever changing. So in some parts of this book you'll see diamond bulleted sections with URL links to articles at www.HomeMusicProduction.com. These articles will contain further information, or the latest updates pertaining to the discussed topic.

## Who is This Book for?

As a passionate home recording musician and hobbyist who uses computer-based tools and recording methods, I've written this book for a similar audience.

I'm guessing that if you're reading this book you are: interested in recording and producing music, just starting to build your recording workstation or looking to expand your current setup, and focused primarily on building a computer-based recording workstation.

I'm also guessing that you're not necessarily a full-time professional music producer nor are you looking to build a full-production recording facility with multiple sound booths and hundreds of thousands of dollars in equipment.

So if you're a singer-songwriter, jazz musician, rock guitarist, classical virtuoso or hip-hop producer looking to successfully record your own music at home, this book is for you.

## What Will You Learn?

This book focuses on the hardware and software needed to produce professional-sounding music at home.

By the end of this book you will learn:

➤ Music production terminology
➤ The hardware you need to produce music
➤ The software you need to produce music
➤ How to incorporate an iPad into your music production setup and workflow
➤ How to set up an ideal recording and mixing environment

You will also get answers to popular questions through FAQs noted in red.

And on that note, let's get on with some home recording studio basics.

Stephan Earl
www.HomeMusicProduction.com

# UNDERSTANDING THE BASICS

In This Chapter:

➢ Terminology

➢ Tools You Will need

## Terminology

Rapid advancements in technology over the last decade or so have opened the doors for home recording enthusiasts to record music from the comfort of our bedrooms and living rooms. We can now produce high-quality recordings comparable to music being recorded in large, dedicated studios. But along with the advancements in technology comes the lingo. Here's some of the terminology discussed throughout this book that you'll want to know, so you can better navigate these waters. If some of the terms look strange or foreign to you now, don't worry they will become second nature to you soon. Here we go:

**A/D:** Analog to digital. A conversion process by which an analog audio signal is converted to a digital signal.

**ADSR:** Attack, Decay, Sustain and Release. An envelope generator present in synthesizers allowing the shaping of a sound's amplitude and filters.

**Aux Send:** Auxiliary Send. An audio signal sent from an individual channel on a mixer to a separate output. This is typically used to send an audio signal to a monitor mix or to trigger effects.

**Band Pass Filter:** An electronic filter which limits the effect of frequencies on either side of a desired frequency range.

**Bit:** Short for Binary Digit. Defines digital audio steps of resolution. Audio CDs use 16-bit resolution or 65,536 steps. DVD-Audio uses 24-bit resolution or 16,777,216 steps, significantly increasing the smoothness and dynamic range of the sound.

**Bouncing:** A technique used in multi-track recording where multiple tracks of recorded audio are combined into a single track.

**Bus:** The routing of an audio input signal to one or more output channels. For example, cymbals, kick drum, snare drum and hi-hat channels can be bussed to a single drum sub-group channel and be controlled by one fader on a mixer.

**Compressor:** An electronic device used to reduce the range of dynamics of an audio signal.

**DAW:** Digital Audio Workstation. Software used with a computer to create music digitally.

**dB:** Decibel (one tenth of a bel). A unit for measuring relative loudness of a sound. dB is a logarithmic scaled measurement named after Alexander Graham Bell. The 0dB position on a mixer is also known as the unity gain position.

**dBFS:** Decibels Below Full Scale. Measures decibel amplitude levels in digital audio.

**DFD:** Direct from Disk (or direct disk streaming). DFD streaming is when a plug-in stores a portion of the required instrument data into RAM, then streams the remaining data from your hard disk drive in real-time.

**Dither:** An intentionally applied form of noise used on 20-bit and higher digital signals before reducing the resolution down to 16-bit. This helps to maintain signal detail when down-sampling to lower bit rates.

**DVI:** Digital Visual Interface. A video interface standard designed to provide very high quality on digital display devices.

**EQ:** Equalization. The electronic balancing of sound frequencies to reduce distortion or achieve a specific effect.

**Filter:** An electronic device that cuts or boosts certain frequencies.

**FireWire:** IEEE 1394 interface. A personal computer and digital video serial bus interface standard that allows high-speed communication between devices.

**Gain:** Refers to the amount of increase or decrease of volume.

**GUI:** Graphic User Interface

**HDD:** Hard Disk Drive. A storage device for digital data.

**Hertz (Hz):** A unit of measurement denoting frequency that is measured in cycles per second.

**Latency:** The delay in time between the input signal and the output signal in an audio chain.

**MIDI:** Musical Instrument Digital Interface. A system designed to transmit information between electronic musical instruments.

**Mbit/s:** Mega-bit per second or 1,000,000 bits per second.

**MB/s:** Mega-byte per second or 8,000,000 bits per second.

**Normalize:** A digital audio process used to raise the level of an audio signal so the loudest peak is at 0 dBFS.

**Out of Phase:** Two signals are out of phase when certain frequencies are cancelled out due to the reversal of polarity of a signal relative to another.

**Panning:** The positioning of an audio signal to the left or right of the stereo panorama.

**Pan-Pot:** Panoramic Potentiometer. A control knob on a mixer used for placing audio signals to the left or right of the stereo panorama.

**Phantom Power:** 48v DC electric power transmitted to a condenser microphone through the microphone cable. Phantom power is typically built into mixing decks and microphone pre-amps.

**RAM:** Random Access Memory. Is a form of computer data storage that is used by software applications and virtual instruments to access data in real time.

**Reverberation:** Also know as Reverb, it's the reflective characteristics of a room. Produced digitally, reverb simulates acoustic characteristics of real spaces such as rooms and halls, or the reflective quality of a large metal plate known as plate reverb.

**RMS:** Root Mean Square. A statistical measure of the magnitude of varying quantity. With digital compressors RMS is typically a setting that attenuates the "average" level of a signal as opposed to attenuating the peaks of the signal.

**Sample:** A portion of a sound that is captured digitally by an electronic device and reused to create new musical work.

**Sequencer:** In today's music production, this typically refers to a software or device that records MIDI data. A MIDI recorder.

**SSD:** Solid-State Drive. A data storage device that uses solid-state memory to store data. This is distinguished from traditional hard disk drives (HDD) which are devices with pinning disks and movable parts.

**SP/DIF:** Sony-Philips Digital Interface. Interface used to carry compressed digital audio using a 75-ohm coaxial RCA cable, or fiber optic TOSLINK connector.

**TOSLINK:** Toshiba Link. Optical audio cable used to carry digital audio.

**Transient:** Used to describe the immediate portion of a sound, including its defining characteristics. For example, the initial pluck of a guitar string.

**USB:** Universal Serial Bus. A personal computer serial bus standard used to establish communication between devices.

**Word Clock:** A clock signal used to synchronize multiple digital devices. This allows you to use one device as the "master" clock in an audio chain for better synchronization, rather than having several devices all running on their own individual clock rates.

# Tools You Will Need

Before you get started, here's a brief summary of the tools needed to make your home music production a success:

## Ergonomic Desk and Chair

Since you'll undoubtedly spend countless hours at your production desk creating and recording music, you'll want a desk space and chair that won't have you feeling fatigued after only a few hours. We'll explore this further in Chapter 7.

## Computer

The heart of your computer-based music production setup will not surprisingly be ... the computer. We'll cover this in some detail in the next chapter, but you'll want to really consider your needs and how the system will be used. We'll look at some the advantages and disadvantages of purchasing a laptop versus a desktop, and will cover some differences between Apple Mac systems versus Windows PCs.

## MIDI Input Device

Once you have the computer sorted, you may want a hardware MIDI controller device to control virtual instruments and effects plug-ins. Depending on your needs and style of music, this item may not be a necessity. For example, if you're only recording external electric or acoustic instruments such as an electric guitar or acoustic piano, then you may not need a MIDI input device. However, if you intend to play and record virtual instruments, then a MIDI controller of some sort is a must.

## Audio Interface

In order to record any professional quality analog audio into your computer, an audio interface is needed. This is basically a professional level sound card that converts the analog signal being recorded to digital code so your computer can process the data. It also does the reverse and converts the digital code from your computer back into analog signals that go to your speakers in order to produce sounds. This is known as the AD/DA conversion process. While most computers come installed with some level of sound card, this is best used for basic music playback and isn't usually sufficient for music production. We'll dive into this further in Chapter 3.

## Digital Audio Workstation (DAW)

If the computer is the heart of a computer-based music production setup, then the DAW is definitely the soul. There are many really great DAWs on the market today and most have very comparable feature sets. The DAW you choose should work with your creative flow and be intuitive to your style of creating. In Chapter 4 we'll take a look at some of the popular DAWs on the market, and I'll provide some suggestions on choosing the right DAW for you.

## Virtual Instruments

One of the great benefits of producing music in this age of technology is the accessibility to a vast array of sounds right from your computer. However, with so many virtual instruments on the market to choose from, it's tough to know which ones may be right for you. In Chapter 5 I'll discuss the generalists and the specialists, or as my mother would say, the jack of all trades versus the master of one. My aim here is to help you spend your precious coin in the right places, because virtual instrument costs can quickly add up, and there is the potential to end up with a virtual lemon.

## Virtual Effects

Virtual effects such as reverb, delay, EQ, compression and limiting are key to achieving that professional sound you're looking for. Fortunately many of the DAWs discussed in this book come out of the box with professional-sounding virtual effects. However, despite your DAWs packaged plug-in set, you may choose to purchase additional third-party plug-in effects and use these in place of the effects that come with your DAW.

## Monitor Speakers/Headphones

Listening to your tracks on professional monitor speakers and headphones during the recording, tracking, mixing and mastering processes is important for achieving a quality product. This doesn't mean you have to spend thousands of dollars on high-end monitors, but you will want to mix your recorded music using monitors designed for professional use and not commercial use.

## Acoustically Controlled Space

The final and arguably most important part of the listening chain is the listening environment itself. In Chapter 7 we'll take a look at room setups and discuss ways to improve the quality of your recordings and mixes by the controlling the acoustics in the room and optimizing the placement of your home recording studio setup.

## Key Points from Chapter 1

- Familiarize yourself with the terms commonly used in music production.
- Start thinking of the items needed to get your home recording studio up and running.

# CHOOSING THE RIGHT COMPUTER

2

In This Chapter:

➤ PC vs. Mac

➤ Laptop vs. Desktop

➤ RAM

➤ CPU

➤ Disk Drives

## PC vs. Mac

Whether you choose a Windows compatible PC or an Apple Mac is a matter of personal preference. Both systems are very capable of providing a smooth music recording experience, so you should take the following points into consideration when making your purchasing decision:

✓ Get familiar with both operating systems. Most popular consumer electronic stores allow you to use and familiarize yourself with the computers on display. The Apple store has an advantage here in that not only can you familiarize yourself with the OS, but you can also play around with Apple's Garage Band and see how you like the DAW within the OS environment.

✓ Your Digital Audio Workstation (DAW) choice will also play a part in which computer you choose. Some DAWs such as Logic and Digital Performer only work on Macs, while others such as FL Studio and Sonar only work with PCs. Spend some time familiarizing yourself with each DAW's environment by reviewing the developer websites and seeing the DAWs in action on YouTube. Once you've narrowed down your choices, peruse forum sites for your DAW choices and select the computer platform with the best feedback for that option.

✓ Consider other music or non-music related software you may want to use. Think about whether or not the computer is compatible with other software you currently own or are considering to purchase.

## Laptop vs. Desktop

Once you've decided on a PC or Mac, then you'll need to consider whether a laptop or a desktop will best serve your music production and home studio needs. There are advantages and disadvantages to both, so you should first ask yourself some discovery questions:

**Are you looking for portability?** Will your home recording computer also be your live performance computer? Do you expect to travel often and want to take your studio with you on planes, tour buses or work from hotel rooms? Will you work with a studio outside of your home studio and potentially record on your system instead of theirs?

**Are you looking for flexibility?** Do you anticipate wanting more than two screen displays? Are you looking to add multiple internal hard drives and DVD drives? Are you looking to customize the computer after purchase? Do you need multiple USB, FireWire or HDMI ports?

**Is computer power and speed most important to you?** Are you looking to have the fastest hard drives and DVD drives available? Are you looking for the most powerful graphics card? Do you anticipate updating the motherboard for future CPU and RAM upgrades?

**What's your budget?** Do you expect to buy another computer in less than two years? Are you looking to avoid buying another computer for five years or more?

Let's take a look at each of these areas as they may help you prioritize your needs.

✓ **Portability:** If you're looking for portability then a laptop is undoubtedly your best option. Laptops come in different flavors from 10" and 13" razor-thin ultrabooks to 17" desktop replacement laptops. With the right CPU and RAM installed, the portability of today's laptops doesn't have to mean a sacrifice in performance.

- ✓ **Flexibility:** If you intend for your computer to live in a recording studio and not move, then you may prefer the flexibility of a desktop. Desktops enable you to upgrade and change components more easily than laptops. Most laptop models only offer limited upgrade capability with components such as RAM, while desktops will allow you to change components such as the graphics card, RAM, additional connection ports and even the motherboard. While upgrading components does require some level of computer-geek savvy, some electronic stores have technical support onsite to assist you with potential upgrades.

One common desktop upgrade is changing the graphics card. If you want three or more external displays, for example, you may need to upgrade the existing graphics card for one with three or more display outputs. You can also achieve this with a desktop or laptop by using a USB external graphics adapter such as the USB2DVIPRO by StarTech ([www.startech.com](www.startech.com)).

- ✓ **Power:** Computer-based music software involves a lot of real-time processing, so a powerful CPU is required whether you want to be mobile or not. Fortunately, the processing power needed to run today's powerful music creation software is available on both laptops and desktops. Your choice here will be primarily driven by your preference for portability versus flexibility… or price.

- ✓ **Budget:** Laptops tend to be more expensive than a desktop of comparable specs. There could often be a $400 to $800 difference between a comparable laptop and desktop, although with a desktop you still have to account for the cost of the monitor(s). If you have limited cash to invest upfront, then a desktop may offer you the ability to buy a model with modest features now and upgrade with more powerful components when you're ready. If you have limited cash upfront and are looking to get a laptop, then you may want to hold off until you have enough of a budget to get the features you need. Otherwise, you may find yourself purchasing a laptop and then requiring a new laptop within a couple of years as you outgrow the first one. This could prove to be more expensive and frustrating than paying for a better system straightaway that lasts longer.

- ❖ For the latest suggestions on music production ready desktops and laptops, visit
http://www.homemusicproduction.com/laptop-vs-desktop-for-home-music-recording/

# RAM

Ram is king in the world of computer-based music production. When choosing a laptop or a desktop computer, you'll want a minimum of 4GB of RAM with the option to upgrade to more. Many powerful laptops come standard with 4GB of RAM with the ability to upgrade to at least 8GB of RAM and many desktops offer upwards of 32GB of RAM. Having the ability to upgrade your RAM will save you money in the long run by avoiding a computer upgrade in two years when your favorite virtual instruments have overextended your current RAM capabilities.

Increased RAM also lessens the need for direct-to-disk streaming by your virtual instruments, improves performance and could eliminate crackling due to disk streaming overload.

Please note that a 64-bit operating system and a DAW that runs in native 64-bit mode are required to take advantage of more than 3GB of RAM.

➤ If you use a 32-bit DAW in a 32-bit OS such as Windows 7 32-bit, your DAW will only access up to 2GB of RAM and your OS will only access up to 3GB of RAM. This is true even if you have more than 3GB of RAM installed in your computer (Mac OS X Lion is a native 64-bit OS and doesn't come in a 32-bit version).

➤ If you use a 32-bit DAW (or a DAW in 32-bit mode) in a 64-bit OS, your DAW will only access 2GB of RAM, but your OS will be able to access remaining RAM for other applications you may have in use. So if you have 8GB of RAM in your system, then 2GB can be accessed by your DAW, and the remaining 6GB can be accessed by the OS to use for other applications.

➤ If you have a 64-bit DAW in a 64-bit OS, your DAW will be able to access all available RAM in your system.

DAWs and sample-based virtual instruments require a lot of RAM in order to ensure smooth real-time playback. It's not uncommon for a virtual instrument such as Synthogy's Ivory II Grand Piano to require 1.5GB of RAM just to play its Steinway D Concert Grand. If you add other sampled instruments such as an acoustic drum kit and an electric bass, you could quickly require over 2GB of RAM just for these few instruments.

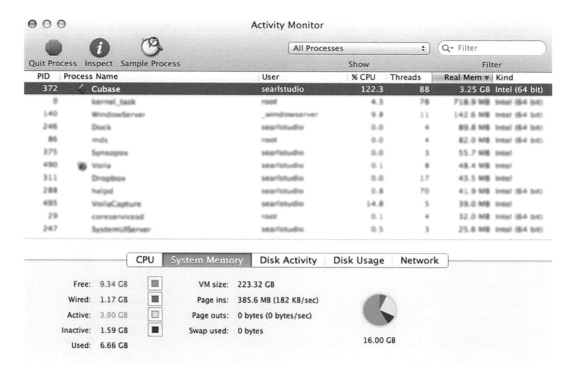

**Figure 2-1:** The Mac OS X Activity Monitor

# CPU

If RAM is king, then the processor or CPU is queen. The second half of the royal computing family is the processor, and more importantly, a multi-core processor. You can read more in-depth on multi-core processors on Wikipedia; however, in the basic sense, consider the core (or processor) as a single brain. One brain can process information well, but it could process even better if duties were divided among four or eight brains. If you're purchasing a new desktop or laptop for music production, you should look for Intel Core i5, Core i7 or AMD Phenom II multi-core processors.

**NOTE**

Figure 2-1 shows my system's available RAM. In this example, the only application I have open is Cubase 6 along with six virtual instruments. I have 16GB of RAM on my system and with no tracks yet recorded, my system is using 6.66GB of RAM for the OS and Cubase. Of that, Cubase is using 3.25GB of RAM just for the application and six instantiated plug-ins with no tracks recorded.

Most popular DAWs such as Logic and Cubase are programmed to take advantage of computers with multi-core processors by dividing the real-time processing functions between the various cores. Not all DAWs on the market are programmed to take advantage of multi-core systems, so research the developer's specifications on the DAW before you purchase it. In both OS X and Windows, you can open the system performance window and see how (or if) your DAW is utilizing all cores on your computer.

While sample-based virtual instruments tend to be RAM needy, virtual effects plug-ins and other DAW real-time processes are very CPU needy. So the more tracks you have playing at the same time with multiple effects plug-ins instantiated per track, the more you run the risk of overworking the CPU. The result of mild CPU overload is crackling, while the result of heavy CPU overload can be software freeze or crashing.

## Disk Drives

Disk drives are next in line of computer importance when it comes to producing music. During the last few years as sample-based instruments have increased in size, disk drives have played an increasingly larger role for a couple of reasons:

1. Sample-based instruments are much more detailed now, with some popular virtual instruments requiring more than 80GB of hard drive space.

2. With a single virtual instrument patch requiring as much as 1.2GB of RAM, developers often implement direct from disk (DFD) or direct disk streaming. DFD streaming is when a plug-in stores a portion of the required instrument data into RAM, then streams the remaining data from your hard disk drive (HDD) in real-time. Since this functionality is often controllable, you can allow more or less data to load into RAM as is best for your system's performance.

One downside to DFD streaming is that it requires your HDD to be fast and uncluttered so the data doesn't get bogged down causing stuttering or crackling performance.

Here are some tips to remember when looking for the right computer and disk drive performance:

**Internal HDD**

Look for an internal HDD with minimum spindle speed of 7200RPM (revolutions per minute). This speed is more commonly found in desktop computers and higher-end laptops. Less expensive laptops tend to have 5400RPM HHDs, so look out for this when purchasing a laptop. The faster drive will benefit you most with plug-ins that feature DFD streaming and audio tracks that are being streamed by your DAW.

Use your computer's internal HDD primarily for the operating system and software such as your DAW, virtual instruments and effects plug-ins. Use a separate HDD (either internal or external) for your DAW project files, audio track files, loop libraries and audio files for sample-based instruments. This will help improve your DAW's playback performance by avoiding a traffic jam caused by a single HDD reading OS data, audio file data and instrument streaming data all at the same time.

If you have a healthy budget for a computer and can purchase a solid-state drive (SSD) as your primary internal hard drive, then this would provide you with the fastest speed currently available. SSDs have no spinning or movable parts, so they're considerably faster then HDDs. Data also doesn't get fragmented on an SSD, allowing complete chunks of data to be accessed quicker. Currently this technology is considerably more expensive than a standard HDD, but like most new technologies will decrease in price in the coming years. Apple currently offers SSD drives as standard on its MacBook Air models, and it is a custom option on its MacBook Pro, iMac and Mac Pro models.

## External HD

External HDDs are considerably less expensive than they were just a few years ago. This means you can purchase a good USB 3.0 7200RPM 2TB external HDD for less than $150. Utilizing an HDD with these specifications to stream your recorded audio track files and sample-based virtual instrument files ensures best performance, especially on larger projects. If you are purchasing a new HDD, go straight for a USB 3.0 HDD and avoid remaining USB 2.0 HDDs. We'll review the performance differences between FireWire, USB2.0 and USB 3.0 in Chapter 3.

### NOTE

Synthogy Ivory II virtual piano requires 77GB of hard disk space and ships on 11 DVD ROM disks. With a fast DVD drive boasting 16x read speed, each disk takes approximately 15 minutes to load, and 2 hours 45 minutes to load the entire library. Many laptops come with an internal DVD drive capable of 8x read speed. This means each disk of Ivory II will take approximately 30 minutes to load, and 5 ½ hours to load the entire library. If you have a desktop, then you may have a DVD ROM drive with a 16x read speed, but if you have a laptop, you could purchase an external DVD ROM drive with a read speed of 32x that will load Ivory in about 1 hour and 12 minutes.

## Optical Drive

With most data and information being accessible from the cloud these days, the need for an optical CD/DVD drive has declined. However, while most applications now have less need for a fast optical drive, the opposite is the case when it comes to loading sample-based virtual instrument libraries. Many of today's popular sample-based virtual instruments by developers like East West, Spectrasonics and Native Instruments contain upwards of 80GB of sampled audio files (110GB of HDD space is required for NI's Komplete 8). Loading these DVDs onto your HDD is very time-consuming, and if you ever need to load all of you instruments onto a new drive, this can often take one to two full days depending on how many large libraries you have. Below is a real-world example.

## Key Points from Chapter 2

- Familiarize yourself with both PC and Mac operating systems before making a purchase decision.
- Laptops allow portability and power, while desktops allow flexibility and power.
- Add as much RAM to your computer as you can afford.
- A computer with quad-core processing is best.
- Install audio file content onto a different HDD than your OS and DAW when possible.
- Solid-state drives cost more, but are faster than HDDs.
- A fast optical CD/DVD drive saves time during instrument installs.

# EXTERNAL AUDIO AND MIDI HARDWARE

In This Chapter:

➢ Audio Interfaces

➢ Guitar Interfaces

➢ MIDI Controllers

➢ Using an iPad as a Controller

➢ Reference Monitors

➢ Cabling

## Audio Interfaces

Once you have a fast and powerful computer ready to produce music, you'll need an audio interface to get the audio in and out of the computer. The audio interface is a very important piece of hardware for recording since it converts your incoming analog audio signal (ex. microphone, electric guitar, external synths) into digital, and converts the computer's digital signal back into analog, so you can hear the sound through your speakers. Virtual instruments are born in the digital world, so they are only converted from digital to analog for your listening. If your audio interface doesn't do a good job of converting, both the recorded audio going in and the audio you hear will be compromised and the mixing and mastering decisions you're making will be less accurate.

There are three types of audio interfaces on the market:

1) FireWire
2) USB
3) PCI

### FireWire Audio Interface
FireWire audio interfaces connect to your computer using a FireWire port. We'll discuss FireWire more in

the next chapter, but it comes in two standards: FireWire 400 (IEEE 1394 4-pin or 6-pin) and FireWire 800 (IEEE 1394b 9-pin). FireWire has a data transfer speed of up to 400 Mb/s. While this on paper is slower than the 480 Mb/s transfer speed of USB 2.0, FireWire delivers faster performance because it has less computer dependencies than USB 2.0, and performs better for sustained data transfers like digital audio.

**Figure 3-1:** The M-Audio FireWire Solo FireWire audio interface

## USB Audio Interface

USB audio interfaces connect to your computer using one of its USB 2.0 or USB 3.0 ports. USB 2.0 has a data transfer speed of 480 Mb/s. While the data transfer speed of USB 2.0 is listed as 480 Mb/s or 60 MB/s, this refers to the burst data speed. The sustained transfer speed is closer to 10-30 MB/s, depending on the data being transferred, speed of the computer and length of USB 2.0 cable.

USB audio interfaces currently feature the USB 2.0 standard, however, in the coming years this will change to the newer USB 3.0 standard, which sports data transfer speeds up to 4 GB/s. As most newer PC laptops no longer ship with FireWire ports, you will more than likely require a USB audio interface if you are purchasing a newer PC or MacBook Air laptop (MacBook Pro, iMac and Mac Pro computers have 9-pin FireWire 800 ports in addition to USB).

## PCI Audio Interface

PCI audio interfaces connect directly to the motherboard of a desktop computer using an available PC slot. While this technology has been replaced by the faster PCI Express (PCIe) technology, it's worth mentioning since PCI audio interfaces are still produced by manufacturers such as MOTU, M-Audio and RME. The aforementioned manufacturers also produce a few PCIe models that take advantage of PCIe's 2.5 Gb/s data transfer rate.

**FAQ:** Do I really need an audio interface? Can't I just use the computer's built-in soundcard?

You will absolutely need an audio interface if you want the best audio input and output from your computer. While built-in computer soundcards are sufficient for basic audio playing, the quality for audio recording is typically poor and you will experience greater levels of MIDI and audio recording latency. Soundcards built into Macs tend to have less latency than soundcards that ship with most PCs, however, this will only be good for basic MIDI recording. If you have a PC and want improved soundcard performance without an audio interface, you can download ASIO4all, which is a free universal ASIO driver for PC.

**FAQ:** Why is all that technical data transfer stuff important?

Latency. Latency is the delay in time between the input signal and the output signal in an audio chain. The slower the data transfer rate is between your audio interface and your computer, the more latency or sound delay you experience.

## SEVEN TIPS TO REDUCE LATENCY

**TIP 1:** To improve the performance of your audio interface, use the shortest length of high-quality cable possible. This will lessen the amount of overhead the transferring data has to navigate through. This is especially true of audio interfaces using USB 2.0.

**TIP 2:** Always download the latest software drivers for your audio interface.

**TIP 3:** If you're using a PC, set your computer to high performance in the "Systems" menu from the Control Panel.

**TIP 4:** Turn off all system sounds. On a PC this is also accessible from the Control Panel in the "Sounds" menu. On a Mac, the "Sounds" menu is accessible from the "System Preferences."

**TIP 5:** On a PC, set processor scheduling to "Background Services." This will improve the performance of your audio drivers. To access this, go to Control Panel > System > Advanced System Settings > Performance. Then select "Background Services" and hit OK.

**TIP 6:** Use some of the tips mentioned in the previous chapter to improve computer performance: Get more RAM and use a fast separate HDD for audio recording.

**TIP 7:** Increase audio buffer on your interface as you increase the number of tracks and for mixing. Generally an audio (ASIO) buffer of 250 is good for general MIDI and audio recording. With a powerful computer and lots of RAM, you can use a buffer of 125, which decreases latency. As you add more tracks, or when you're ready for mix-down, you can increase your audio buffer to 500 or higher.

# Guitar Interfaces

If you're a guitarist, you have a few options for getting your acoustic, electric or bass guitar's audio into the computer: You can use a standard audio interface or one of the growing numbers of analog and digital guitar interfaces on the market.

Here are some popular methods to get your acoustic, electric or bass guitar's audio into your computer:

➢ **Method 1**: Guitar > favorite amp > microphone > audio interface > computer

➢ **Method 2**: Guitar > audio interface > computer

➢ **Method 3**: Guitar > analog guitar interface > mobile device or computer

➢ **Method 4**: Guitar > digital USB guitar interface > mobile device or computer

**Method 1:** Using a good quality dynamic or condenser microphone in an acoustically controlled space will enable you to mic your acoustic guitar or guitar amp and send a fantastic tone to your computer. Connect your microphone into the audio interface using a high-quality balanced audio cable and you're ready to record (see Figure 3-2).

**Method 2:** This is the most popular method for recording guitars. Using guitar amp emulation software such as Native Instruments' Guitar Rig, IK Multimedia's AmpliTube and Peavey's ReValver, most guitarists are happy to create their perfect guitar tones "in the box." Start with a high-quality ¼" audio cable connected directly from your guitar to your USB or FireWire audio interface. Load your DAW and instantiate the guitar amp plug-in of your choice, and you're ready to record (see Figure 3-3).

**Method 3:** With the advent of the iPhone, iPad and Android devices, manufacturers and software developers have created portable guitar interfaces that enable you to plug your guitar directly into these mobile devices. These interfaces often come bundled with guitar amp emulation software comparable to guitar amp emulation plug-ins for your DAW. This method features an analog guitar interface, which means the output is usually a stereo mini connector that plugs into the headphone jack of your mobile device, or into your computer audio interface. (See Figure 3-4 for an example of an analog guitar interface.)

**Method 4:** Lastly, you can use a digital guitar interface such as NI's Guitar Rig Kontrol to connect your guitar to a computer or mobile device via a USB cable or Apple's 3-pin connector. Like their analog counterparts, these digital guitar interfaces often come bundled with amp emulation software. The advantage of a digital guitar interface is that the signal path to the computer or mobile device is digital, so there's no loss of audio quality. One disadvantage to these interfaces is that it may be limited to connecting your guitar to an iPhone or iPad using Apple's 30-pin connector. Below is a listing of popular analog and digital guitar interfaces with a description of how they connect your guitar to a computer or mobile device. (See Figure 3-5 for an example of a USB audio interface.)

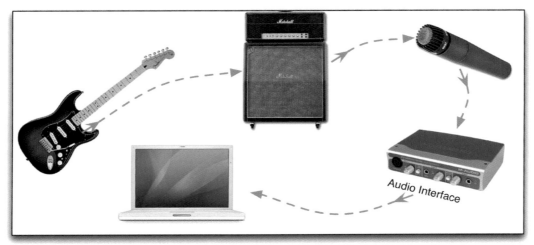

**Figure 3-2:** Method 1. The electric guitar is connected to the guitar amp. A dynamic mic picks up the sound and sends it to the audio interface.

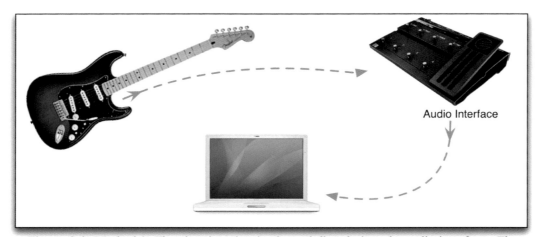

**Figure 3-3:** Method 2. The electric guitar is plugged directly into the audio interface. The audio interface sends the sound via USB directly to the computer.

## Popular Guitar Interfaces

More and more recording manufacturers and software developers are producing interfaces designed specifically for use with guitars. Here's a listing of some popular analog and digital interfaces:

- **AcousticLink** (www.alesis.com): AcousticLink by Alesis is a digital acoustic guitar to USB interface. AcousticLink contains an easy-to-install acoustic guitar pickup and a ¼" to USB cable to connect your acoustic guitar to any Mac or PC.

- **AmpKit LiNK** (www.peavey.com): AmpKit LiNK by Peavey is an analog guitar interface that includes amp emulation software. Use a ¼" audio cable to plug your guitar into the device. The attached mini stereo plug connects to your mobile device, and there's a mini stereo jack to plug in your headphones. The headphone jack gives you the post-amp effected sound, so use this to connect to your computer audio interface if you want to record the effected guitar tone into your computer DAW.

- **GiO** (www.peavey.com): GiO by Apogee is a digital guitar and audio interface designed for use with Garage Band and Logic Pro. GiO combines an audio interface, effects stomp pedalboard controller and DAW controller all in one (see Figure 3-5). Use a ¼" audio cable to plug your guitar to the pedalboard interface, and use a USB cable to connect the interface to your Mac.

- **Guitar Link UCG102** (www.behringer.com): Guitar Link UCG102 by Behringer is a digital guitar interface that includes amp emulation software. Use a ¼" audio cable to plug your guitar into the device, and plug the attached USB cable into your Mac or PC.

- **Guitar Rig Kontrol** (www.native-instruments.com): Guitar Rig Kontrol by Native Instruments is a digital guitar and audio interface that includes a full version of Guitar Rig Pro amp emulation software. Guitar Rig Kontrol combines an audio interface, guitar effects pedalboard controller and expression pedal. Use a ¼" audio cable to plug your guitar to the pedalboard interface, and use a USB cable to connect the interface to your Mac or PC.

- **iJam** (www.rapcohorizon.com): iJam by RapcoHorizon is a 3-in-1 analog interface, practice amplifier and MP3 play-along device. Use a ¼" audio cable to plug your guitar into the device. Use the built-in stereo mini plug jack to plug in your headphones or output to your computer audio interface.

- **iRig** ([www.ikmultimedia.com](www.ikmultimedia.com)): iRig by IK Multimedia is an analog guitar interface that includes a mobile version of AmpliTube. Use a ¼" audio cable to plug your guitar into the device. At the opposite end is a mini stereo plug to connect to your mobile device and a mini stereo jack to plug in your headphones. The headphone jack gives you the post-amp effected sound, so use this to connect to your computer audio interface if you want to record the effected guitar tone into your computer DAW (see Figure 3-4).

- **Jam** ([www.apogeedigital.com](www.apogeedigital.com)): Jam by Apogee is a digital guitar interface that works exclusively with iPhone, iPad and Mac. Use a ¼" audio cable to plug your guitar into the device. Jam comes with both a USB cable for connection to a Mac, and a USB to 30-pin connector cable for connection to an iPhone or iPad.

- **Mobile In** ([www.line6.com](www.line6.com)): Mobile In by Line 6 is a digital guitar interface that includes amp emulation software. Use a ¼" audio cable to plug your guitar into the device, and it connects digitally to an iPhone or iPad using Apple's 30-pin connector.

- **X-port** ([www.peavey.com](www.peavey.com)): X-port by Peavey is a digital guitar interface that includes amp emulation software. Use a ¼" audio cable to plug your guitar into the device, and a USB cable to connect it into your Mac or PC.

**Figure 3-4:** The IK Multimedia iRig. This analog guitar interface features a mobile version of AmpliTube amp simulation software.

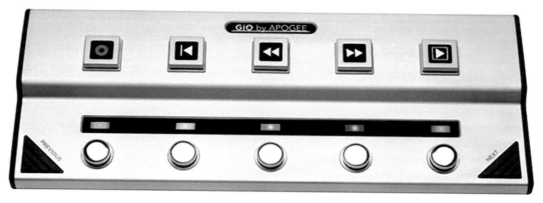

**Figure 3-5:** The Apogee GiO USB audio interface features a built-in effects stomp pedalboard and DAW controller and works with Garage Band and Logic Pro.

❖ For the latest information on guitar interfaces and amp emulation software, visit http://www.homemusicproduction.com/guitar-interface-and-amp-emulation-software-round-up.

# MIDI Controllers

With the audio interface taken care of, it's time to consider what MIDI device(s) you may want to use to record notes and/or control various functions of your music software.

MIDI, which stands for Musical Instrument Digital Interface, is the industry-standard protocol invented in the early '80s that enables electronic instruments, controllers and computers to communicate with each other. Initially, the only cable used for MIDI was the 5-pin connector cable that is still used today (see figure 3-6). However, other cable formats including USB and FireWire are now also used to send MIDI messages between devices. So consider that MIDI now refers to the message protocol and not necessarily a type of cable.

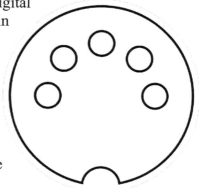

**Figure 3-6:** The MIDI DIN 5/180° connector

There are many controllers on the market that take advantage of MIDI. For keyboardists and general note input, there are MIDI keyboard controllers. For wind players, there are wind controllers. To trigger drum sounds or to trigger audio samples, there are drum controllers. There are controllers to control your DAW, virtual instrument and virtual effects plug-ins, and there's the iPad and other mobile devices that can perform all of the tasks mentioned above. Let's take a closer look at each these controllers.

## Keyboard Controller

MIDI keyboard controllers are not only used by keyboardists, but also by musicians, DJs and producers of all styles of music who are looking for an easy way control their virtual instruments, play melodies and chords, tap out rhythms and trigger samples.

If you are a pianist, you may decide to purchase a MIDI keyboard that has 88 keys with a hammer-action feel. This will feel closest to playing an acoustic grand piano. If you're not a pianist, you may want to get a 25-, 49- or 61-key MIDI keyboard with either a light-action or a semi-weighted feel. Light-action (or synth-action) means when you press on the keys the feel is very light and easy to play. It's the standard feel of the classic synthesizers from the '80s. Semi-weighted action is a slightly heavier feel between light-action and the heavier hammer-action.

Some MIDI keyboard controllers also feature drum pads (or trigger pads), transport controls, faders and rotary encoders that enable you control of your DAW, virtual instruments and virtual effects (see Figure 3-7). This type of all-in-one controller is a great choice if you're looking for a simplified setup with maximum control.

**Figure 3-7:** The M-Audio Axiom 49 MKII semi-weighted MIDI controller.

## Wind Controller

MIDI wind controllers are well suited for instrumentalists who play wind instruments such as: trumpet, saxophone, clarinet, oboe, flute, recorder or other wind instruments. MIDI wind controllers are often referred to as EWI (pronounced Eee-wee), named after the popular Electronic Wind Instrument manufactured by Akai.

Popular wind controllers for woodwind players include Yamaha's WX5 and Akai's EWI 4000s and EWI USB. Both the WX5 and the EWI USB are purely MIDI controllers that connect to your computer. The WX5 connects to your computer via a DIN 5/180° MIDI Out (see Figure 3-6), and the EWI USB connects via a USB cable. The EWI 4000s connects to your computer using a DIN 5/180° MIDI cable. It also comes with a built-in analog modeled synthesizer that connects to the audio input on your audio interface or any analog audio system using a ¼" audio cable. All three of these wind controllers allow you to program different note fingerings to emulate the note fingerings of acoustic instruments including a saxophone or flute.

Trumpet players can check out the Morrison Digital Trumpet (MDT) wind controller. This controller connects via a DIN 5/180° MIDI cable, uses trumpet note fingering and is available for purchase at Patchman Music (www.patchmanmusic.com).

Since these instruments connect to your computer via the DIN 5/180° MIDI cable (with the exception of the EWI USB), you'll either need an audio interface with a DIN 5/180° MIDI In, or a separate USB to MIDI interface such as the Roland UM-1EX MIDI interface or the M-Audio UNO.

**Figure 3-8:** The Akai EWI USB Electronic Wind Instrument

## Guitar Controller

Electric guitarists and bassists have a couple of options to record MIDI into a computer. The first is to use a MIDI guitar controller, and the second option is to use a guitar-to-MIDI interface system.

Guitar and bass MIDI controllers look, feel and play just like standard electric guitar and bass instruments. However, in addition to having a standard audio output connector, they also have digital audio-to-MIDI pickups that send MIDI signals via built-in MIDI ports. Guitar MIDI controllers currently are manufactured by companies such a Fender and Godin. Industrial Radio makes the MIDI Bass that comes in standard and deluxe models.

A guitar-to-MIDI interface system uses digital MIDI guitar pickups that attach to any electric guitar or bass, and sends the audio signal to a separate converter box that converts the audio signal to MIDI data. A popular guitar-to-MIDI interface system is the Roland GI-20 (see Figure 3-9).

Both options will allow you to record guitar audio and MIDI data to your DAW simultaneously, however, one advantage of the guitar-to-MIDI interface system is the ability to use your favorite electric guitar or bass.

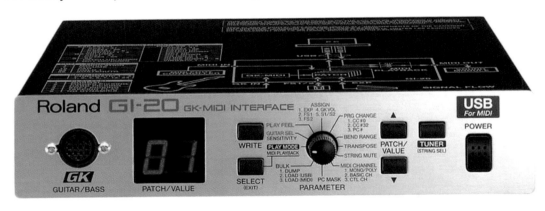

**Figure 3-9:** The Roland GI-20 GK MIDI Interface detects the signal from any electric guitar or bass equipped with a GK-2A or 2B pickup, respectively, and lets you play synthesizers and samplers and record MIDI into your DAW.

## Drum Controller

Drum controllers come in two varieties: electronic drum kits and MIDI drum pad controllers.

Electronic drum kits resemble traditional acoustic drum kits and are primarily designed for drummers. Many of these kits contain a built-in tone generator with high-quality sample and/or synthetic drum sounds. In addition, these kits come with USB or DIN 5/180° MIDI connectivity, allowing you very detailed control of computer virtual drum instrument sounds and articulations (see Figure 3-10).

MIDI drum pad controllers often resemble standard drum machines with 12 or 16 soft rubber drum pads. These controllers contain highly sensitive velocity pads, and are great for tapping out drum rhythms. If you're not a keyboardist, you may find creating drum patterns with a pad controller preferable to using a piano keyboard.

Pad controllers are also very popular with DJs and producers for triggering non-drum sounds and effects. Since a drum pad can typically be assigned to trigger either a MIDI note or a MIDI controller event, such as volume, reverb, delay, etc., these are popular for triggering samples, virtual effects or even entire songs.

**Figure 3-10:** The Yamaha DTX900k Electronic Drum Kit includes built-in drum sounds and is a complete MIDI controller.

**Figure 3-11:** The Korg nanoPAD2 MIDI pad controller includes 16 velocity sensitive pads and an X-Y touchpad.

## Studio Controller

Studio controllers offer tactile control of your music production software and effects, and free you up from having to consistently use your computer keyboard and mouse while recording or performing live. They can be as simple and inexpensive as a Korg NanoKontrol MIDI controller for $59, or as elaborate as an Avid System 5-MC for $133,000.

One popular studio controller is a DAW control surface. This controller resembles an audio mixing board and can be as small as a single-channel controller or as large as a 48-channel controller. DAW control surfaces connect to your computer with either a USB or FireWire cable, and use MIDI mapping protocols such as the MCU (Mackie Control Universal) or HUI (Human User Interface) protocols to communicate with your DAW. These MIDI mapping protocols simply allow your DAW and hardware control surface to exchange MIDI signals that synchronize the virtual and hardware faders, sliders, buttons, wheels and displays (see Figure 3-12).

Another type of popular studio controller is a DJ digital controller. DJ controllers connect to your computer via USB and allow you to control DJ performance and recording software. These controllers enable you to emulate classic DJ performance techniques as cross fading, scratching, pitch and level controls, and headphone previewing without the use of a mouse.

**Figure 3-12:** Avid Artist Mix control surface features touch-sensitive motorized faders, rotary encoders, programmable buttons and EuCon, an ethernet high-speed control protocol developed by Euphonix.

# Using an iPad as a Controller

If you're looking for a good all-purpose controller, Apple's iPad is quickly growing as the controller of choice for many musicians, producers and DJs. As of this writing there are more than 250,000 applications created specifically for the iPad and many of them focus on music performance and control. Useful control apps for the iPad include: DJ control apps, DAW control surface apps, keyboard and other instrument control apps, and drum pad control apps.

One advantage to using an iPad as a music production controller is that you only need to purchase one piece of hardware. Then you can load it up with different applications to do the same work as multiple dedicated hardware controllers. Another advantage of the iPad is that most of these controller apps connect wirelessly to your computer. This frees you of wires and allows you to control your setup remotely from across the room. If you prefer the stability of a wired connection, many of these apps offer that as well.

Here are some iPad controller apps that are worth checking out:

- **AC-7 Core** (www.saitarasoftware.com): AC-7 control surface app by Saitara Software turns your iPad into a wireless multi-touch hardware control surface for your DAW software. AC-7 connects wirelessly to your PC or MAC using Saitara's rtpMIDI driver for the PC, or CoreMIDI for the Mac. It has a nice GUI (Graphic User Interface) and features native control of most popular DAWs.

- **djay** (www.algoriddim.com): There are a plethora of DJ apps for the iPad. However, djay for iPad by algoriddim is an Apple Design Award winner, and when you take a look at this app, you'll see why. The GUI is crisp and functional and the app features all the DJ controls you'd expect (scratching, mixing, pitch control, etc.) and some that are quite unique.

- **Lemur** (www.liine.net): The iOS version of the discontinued Jazz Mutant Lemur. Now produced by Liine, the Lemur iOS controller app allows you to create a plug-in or DAW controller app that is specific to your needs. Programming Lemur can range from fairly easy for a simple controller to very complex using script programming. You use graphic objects in multiple shapes and styles to create your own unique multi-touch control interface, and then assign these objects to any note or MIDI control message on your DAW. This app requires some time to learn, but is well worth the effort.

- **TouchAble** (www.touch-able.com): If you use or are considering Ableton Live as your music production recording platform, then this app is certainly worth a look. It features wireless control of many common features within Ableton Live, and the GUI is well designed.

- **TouchOSC** (www.hexler.net): TouchOSC by Hexler is a modular MIDI control surface app that allows you to design MIDI controllers for pretty much any function you like. It works by sending and receiving OSC (Open Sound Control) messages wirelessly (or wired) to your computer that can then be converted to MIDI. Similar to Lemur, you use graphic objects in multiple shapes and styles to create your own unique multi-touch control interface, and then assign these objects to any note or MIDI control message on your DAW. This app has a fairly steep requires some time to learn

See the section in Chapter 6, "Using an iPad for Music Production," for more information on iPad music production apps and setup.

# Microphones

If you're planning to record your voice or an acoustic instrument into your DAW, then you'll need a microphone to get sound into your computer. The three most common types of microphones for studio recording and live performance are: dynamic, condenser and ribbon. Mics can also be either analog or digital, and can have different polarity (or sound pick up) patterns.

The type, brand and model of mic you choose will be determined by several factors, including how you intend to use it, the style of music and your personal preferences. Since there is no one-mic-fits-all solution, I recommend you first narrow down the type of mic needed based on the information below, then spend some time at your local music store listening to your voice or instrument through a few different microphones. Now let's look at some of the various types of mics out there.

## Understanding Microphone Polarity

The first thing to understand about microphones is the polarity, or the pattern of sound pick up. The three most common polarity types are: omnidirectional, cardioid (directional) and figure-8 (bidirectional).

**Omnidirectional:** Omnidirectional mics pick up sounds 360° around them. A mic with this pick-up pattern is good for recording ambient spaces such as outside nature recording, inside room ambience, and choir and orchestra music (see Figure 3-13).

**Cardioid:** A cardioid mic picks up sounds in front of it, and avoids sounds behind. A mic with this pick-up pattern is good for live performance, because it focuses on sound coming from the voice or instrument in front of the mic and avoids sounds from the other instruments (see Figure 3-14).

**Figure-8:** Figure-8 mics pick up sounds in front and behind, and avoid sound from the sides. A mic with this pattern is good for recording two vocalists or instruments with one mic, while avoiding others instruments (see Figure 3-15).

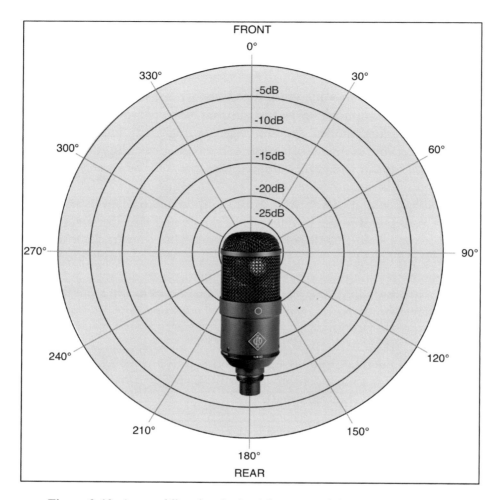

**Figure 3-13:** An omnidirectional mic picks up sound that is 360° around it.

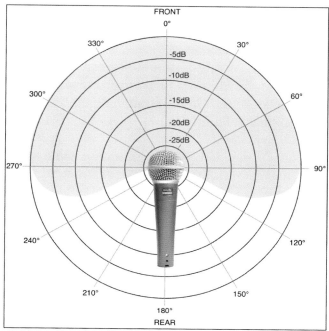

**Figure 3-14:** A cardioid (or directional) mic picks up sound that is in front of it, but not behind it.

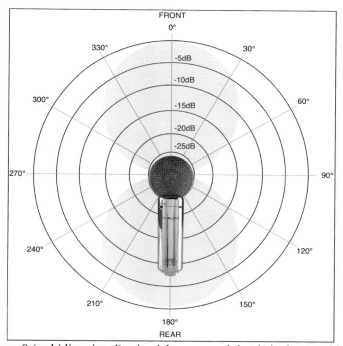

**Figure 3-15:** A figure-8 (or bidirectional) mic picks up sound that is in front and behind it, but not to the sides.

## Analog vs. USB Microphones

An analog mic converts acoustic sound into electrical signals, and uses a 3-pin XLR or ¼" audio cable to connect to your audio hardware. Analog mic signals are generally too weak to transmit sound to your audio recording hardware or software, so they require preamplifiers (or mic preamps) to increase the signal enough to be sufficient for recording. Audio interfaces have mic preamps built into them, so for most home recording needs, you would simply connect your mic to the audio interface via an audio cable (see Figure 3-16).

USB mics convert acoustic sound to digital information using a built-in A/D (analog to digital) converter. They also have built-in mic preamps, so this allows them to be connected directly to your computer using only a USB cable (see Figure 3-17). Also, because the signal is digital, there's less chance of picking up noise, so the signal to noise ratio is greater.

One limitation of using a USB mic for music production is that some DAWs can only use one audio driver at a time to record audio. So without some advanced level tinkering, you may not be able to record your USB mic within your DAW while using a separate audio interface.

> ❖ Mac OS X allows you to combine multiple audio interfaces and USB audio devices by creating an "Aggregate Device". Visit http://www.homemusicproduction.com/using-multiple-audio-interfaces-and-audio-devices-in-mac-os-x/ to learn more.

**Figure 3-16:** An analog dynamic mic sends the audio signal to the audio interface via a 3-pin XLR or ¼" audio cable. The audio interface, with built-in preamp, sends the signal to the computer via a USB or FireWire cable. The computer sends the combined audio signal back to the audio interface through the same USB or FireWire cable. The audio interface sends the final audio output to the speakers via ¼" audio cables.

**Figure 3-17:** A digital USB mic sends the audio signal directly to the computer via a USB cable. The computer sends the final audio output from your recording software to your headphones or speakers via a stereo mini plug.

# FAQ: Is an analog or USB mic right for me?

## A USB mic is right for you if:

✓ You're using the mic primarily for podcasting, video tutorials or voiceover work.
✓ You're using headphones or speakers that plug directly into the computer using its internal soundcard.

## An analog mic is right for you if:

✓ You have a full home recording studio with a need for multiple mic inputs, MIDI input devices, electric guitar or bass, and virtual instruments.
✓ You're using an audio interface for above-mentioned inputs.
✓ You're using professional monitor speakers with ¼" inputs.

Some good USB mics to consider for podcasting, video tutorials and voiceovers are:

• **Audio-Technica AT2020USB** ($150): This USB cardioid mic is popular among podcasters. It's affordable and has a natural well-balanced sound.

- **Rode Podcaster** ($230): The Podcaster mic was based on the Broadcaster mic also by Rode. The frequency response on this mic was designed specifically for direct-to-computer podcasting and voice-overs.

- **Blue Microphones Yeti Pro** ($250): I happen to like Blue mics if for no other reason then they look very cool. Don't get me wrong -- they're also well-made and sound great. The Yeti Pro condenser mic stands out for its great sound, USB and XLR output, and four pick-up patterns (omnidirectional, cardioid, bidirectional and stereo).

- **MXL USB 009** ($300): The 009 is a high-end 24-bit 96 kHz condenser USB mic with amazing detail and built-in rotary knobs for gain, mix and headphone controls.

## Dynamic Microphones

Dynamic mics are rugged, can handle high volume and are resistant to moisture, making them a good fit for live performance. They have a limited frequency response and don't represent high frequencies very well. For this reason you don't typically find dynamic mics being used in the studio for vocals or instruments with high frequency ranges, unless the producer is going for a specific sound.

Dynamic mics work by sound entering through the windscreen of the mic and moving a coil that's attached to the diaphragm. The coil is surrounded by an electromagnetic field and it moves when the diaphragm vibrates. This creates a signal flow.

Some good dynamic mics to consider are:

- **Shure SM57** ($80): If you think you only want one dynamic mic to start out with for instrument recording, this may be the one you look at first. This mic is a standard for studio recording and live performance and is very inexpensive. It works especially well for miking for kicks, snares, toms, and guitar amps.

- **Shure SM58** ($90): Likewise, if you only plan to start out with only one dynamic mic for live or studio vocals, the SM58 is a good place to start. It's the industry standard for miking vocals on stage, and is sometimes used for recording vocals in the studio as well.

- **Sennheiser e609** ($110): This dynamic supercardioid mic is a good alternative to the SM57. It's designed well for loud instruments and miking guitar amps.

- **Electro-Voice RE20** ($430):  The RE20 is a dynamic cardioid mic that has been a long-time favorite for voice-over work.  It's virtually free of the bass boosting "proximity effect" when used up close.

---

# FAQ: Is a dynamic mic right for me?

Yes, if you are recording:

✓ **Vocals.**  While a condenser mic is most common for recording vocals, a dynamic mic with its limited frequency response will be a good choice if you want a grungier sound.  Also since dynamic mics tend to be less sensitive than condenser mics, it may be a better choice if you're recording vocals in a noisy room.

✓ **An electric guitar or bass amp.**  A dynamic mic will work well for this application.  If you're looking to capture higher frequencies from the guitar tone, then you can alternatively use a small diaphragm condenser mic.

✓ **Kick, snare, toms.**  A dynamic mic is most common for these instruments.  A large diaphragm mic could also work well.

---

## Condenser Microphones

Condenser mics are very sensitive to sound, and pick up a lot more detail than dynamic mics.  The high frequency response of these mics makes them a popular choice in the studio for recording vocals and other instruments where detailed transient pick up is required.

Condenser (or capacitor) mics have a plate and a thin metal diaphragm with voltage between them.  A signal is created when sound passes through the plate and diaphragm, and voltage is applied causing the diaphragm to vibrate.  The voltage is typically supplied using batteries, or more commonly using "phantom power," which is a low 48V DC current that is sent through the microphone from other sound equipment such as audio mixers or audio interfaces.

The diaphragms in condenser mics generally come in one of two sizes: small (1/2") or large (1"). Large diaphragm condenser mics are more common and respond well to lower frequencies. Small diaphragm mics respond well to higher frequencies and are generally a good choice for instruments with high-frequency content such as flutes, violins, cymbals and hi-hats.

Below are some good condenser mics to consider within the $300 price range. Keep in mind that more expensive won't always mean better sounding. Consider a trip to your local music store to audition as many mics as possible:

- **Audio Technica AT4040** ($300): This large diaphragm condenser mic is a solid choice or recording vocals, acoustic guitars or percussion. A good small diaphragm condenser mic by AT is the ATM450 ($250).

- **AKG Perception 420** ($250): This is a good multi-pattern large diaphragm condenser mic that has three selectable polar patterns – omnidirectional, cardioid and figure-8. It's a good sounding mic with a moderate price tag.

- **Rode NT1-A** ($230): The NT1-A is a popular large diaphragm condenser mic with low noise. It's good for soft acoustic instruments and vocals. A good small diaphragm condenser mic by Rode is the NT5-S ($220).

- **Studio Projects C1** ($250): This is a great sounding large diaphragm condenser mic for vocals. This mic is one you will want to check out.

- ✓ **Cymbals, drum overheads and drum room ambience.** A small diaphragm mic works best for these instruments.
- ✓ **Percussion.** Small and large diaphragm mics are best depending on the register of the instrument.


## Ribbon Microphones

Ribbon microphones were popular in radio broadcasting in the early 20th century, however, they have generally been replaced in the studio by condenser mics. They're very fragile mics with a low output, so a high-gain preamp is required. Ribbon mics tend to be much more expensive than dynamic and condenser mics, so I won't devote much time to them. I will, however, note that these mics have a warm sound, and like other vintage gear from the past, appear to be experiencing somewhat of a renaissance.

# FAQ: Is a condenser mic right for me?

Yes, if you are recording:

✓ **Vocals.** A large diaphragm mic works well for vocals in most situations. A small diaphragm mic is good if you're going for a brighter sound.

✓ **Acoustic guitar.** A large diaphragm mic is a good choice here.

✓ **Violin, acoustic bass and other stringed instruments.** A small diaphragm mic is a good option.

✓ **Piano.** Small and large diaphragm mics are used to record piano. You may want to use the large diaphragm mic for the main body of the piano, and use the small diaphragm mic for the upper register or room ambience.

✓ **Horns and woodwinds.** Depending on the register of the instrument, you may decide to use a small or large diaphragm mic for horns and wind instruments. General rule is to use a small diaphragm for instruments with a higher upper register and a large diaphragm mic for instruments in the mid- and lower registers. For example, your best bet is a large diaphragm mic for trumpets and saxophones, but a small diaphragm mic for flutes.

# FAQ: Is a ribbon mic right for me?

**Maybe.** Creating and recording music is an art and not a science, so feel free to use whatever you feel is best for your music. With that said, dynamic and condenser mics will do just fine for most home recording needs. Take the money saved and put it into other areas of your studio.

**FAQ:** What mics should I have if I plan on recording a band in my home studio?

If you're recording a live band, you may want to consider having at least the following mics in your arsenal:

✓ One good large diaphragm condenser mic for vocals (two if you play acoustic guitar while singing).

✓ Some dynamic mics for recording guitar and bass amps, kick, snare, and toms.

✓ A couple of small diaphragm condenser mics for drum overheads.

## Getting the Best Microphone Sound

No matter what microphone you choose, there are some basic guidelines you should be aware of in order to achieve a good sound.

✓ **Get a good quality microphone.** It all starts here. Get the best quality mic that you can afford and that sounds good to you.

✓ **Use only high-quality shielded cables and the shortest length possible.** Shielded cables reduce the amount of electrical noise from electric cables and other electric sources. Also, high-quality cables often use better materials that could improve the quality of the signal.

✓ **Place the mic within six to 12 inches of its sound source.** While you may see vocalists eating the mic during live shows, this isn't a good practice for studio recording. Condenser mics especially. They're more sensitive to sound than dynamic mics and don't typically handle very high volume signals. So position a studio condenser mic about 12 inches from its source. Dynamic mics can comfortably sit about six inches from the sound source.

✓ **Use a pop filter when recording vocals.** A pop filter is a nylon screen that goes between the mic and the vocalist to reduce the "pop" sound. This is a must-have if you're recording vocals. Fortunately, you can pick these up inexpensively for about $35.

✓ **Control your acoustic environment as much as possible.** Getting the mic as close as possible to the sound source will help. Other good inexpensive methods include: recording in rooms with carpeting and curtains, using closets and installing acoustic foam panels. If you're primarily doing desktop recording for podcasts and voice-overs, you can make a portable sound booth by purchasing four acoustic treatment foam squares and gluing them inside of a box (see Figure 3-18). We'll talk more about acoustic room treatment in Chapter 7.

✓ **Record the signal at or as close to 0dB as possible.** When using a mic to record, you want to capture the loudest signal possible without it distorting or clipping. The sweet spot in digital recording is to keep the recorded signal at or a few dB under 0dB. Start by getting a good signal into your DAW using the input volume controls on your audio interface. You can also utilize insert effects such as limiters and compressors to control the audio peaks.

**Figure 3-18:** You can make your own portable sound booth that works great for minimizing unwanted outside noise while recording podcasts, voice-overs and video tutorials.

# Reference Monitors

The last piece of hardware needed in your music production chain is a pair of monitor speakers and/or monitor headphones. What you want from a good pair of monitors is to get the most accurate possible representation of your music. Simply put, the characteristics of your monitor speakers will color everything you record and mix.

So what should you look for in a good pair of monitors? The first and most important thing to look for is a **neutral tonal balance**. The less color, accentuated bass or accentuated highs the speakers have, the better chance you have of creating a balanced mix. This is one big differentiator between professional near-field studio monitors and consumer hi-fi speakers. Most hi-fi speakers from a consumer electronics store tend to feature increased highs or bass that is advertised to "enhance" the sound of the music. This is exactly what you want to avoid. If the speakers you are listening to have enhanced bass, you will tend to lower the bass in your mixes. The opposite goes for speakers with enhanced high frequencies.

**Get active monitors rather than passive monitors.** Active monitors are self-powered speakers and passive monitors require a separate amplifier. Amplifiers have the potential to further color the sound, so short of getting high-end professional amplifiers, you're better off getting active studio monitors. A pair of active monitors with a 4" to 8" woofer will be sufficient for home recording studios.

**Listen before you buy.** Before purchasing monitors, head to your nearest music store and listen to a few pairs before making a purchase. Bring a CD or MP3 player of music that you are very familiar with, and spend some time listening to the various makes and models in the store. After you've purchased a pair and set them up in your studio, you should again spend time listening to your favorite music through these speakers to familiarize yourself with how they sound in your studio space.

**Also invest in studio headphones and consumer grade computer speakers.** Keep in mind the average listener will hear your music through computer speakers, headphones or a moderate home sound system. For this reason, when you're ready to mix down your tracks, listen to the mix though different references, as well as your high-end speakers, so your music sounds great in all locations. Cars also come equipped with some of the most advanced sound systems out there, so take your mix to your car to see how it sounds there.

# TIPS TO OPTIMIZE YOUR MONITORING

To summarize, you should look for active monitor speakers with 4" to 8" woofers, 55 Hz (or lower) to 20 kHz frequency response, and a neutral tonal balance. Also use studio headphones and computer speakers as alternate references. Here are some other tips to help you get the best monitor reference:

**TIP 1:** Place your monitor speakers either on speaker stands designed to hold studio speakers, or rest them on foam in order to prevent exaggerated bass response.

**TIP 2:** Avoid placing your speakers in corners, since this will enhance the perceived bass.

**TIP 3:** Place your monitors at a distance apart from each other that is equal to their distance from the listening position, creating an equilateral triangle (see Figure 3-19). This will give you a clear representation of the stereo field and allow you to place tracks correctly in the panorama.

**TIP 4:** Always listen to music at low volumes and protect your ears. It's OK to pump it up for short periods of time, but listening at a loud volume for an extended period of time can cause long-term damage, which will not enhance your future music enjoyment!

**TIP 5:** Invest in professional studio headphones and not consumer models. Consumer-grade headphones (similar to consumer-grade speakers) typically enhance the lower and upper frequencies. Headphones such as Sony's MDR series or comparable AKG models will work well.

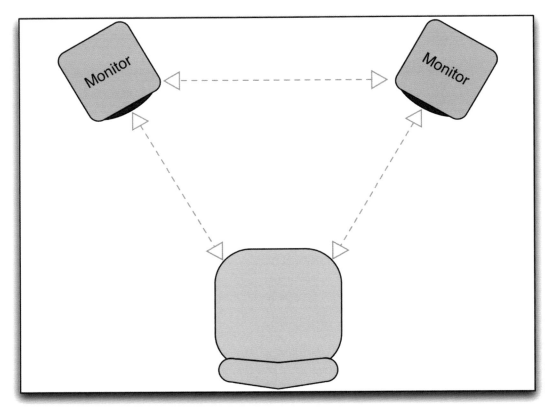

**Figure 3-19:** For the best speaker placement, each studio monitor should sit at an equal distance away from you as they are from each other, creating an equilateral triangle.

# Cabling

Cabling is an essential component of getting a good sound out of your home recording studio. There are a couple of good rules of thumb that will apply to all of the cables you'll need to get your home recording studio up and running. First, use the best quality cables you can for the job. Second, keep the cable run as short as possible.

Whether a cable is analog, digital or electrical, they all have one thing in common: They carry information or current from one device to another. High-quality analog cables use more conductive metals, making it easier for audio signals to travel through. They also have shielding which will protect the traveling audio signal from electrical interferences that can cause noise in your system. High-quality digital cables will ensure the highest possible data transfer speed. Keeping the cable run as short as possible decreases the chance of electrical interference in audio cables and decreases latency (or delay) with digital cables.

Here is some specific information of cables most commonly used in a home recording studio:

## USB

The Universal Serial Bus (USB) cable is the most common cable used in the home recording studio. USB currently comes in two standards, USB 2.0 and USB 3.0. USB 2.0 was released in 2000 and is capable of maximum data transfer speeds up to 480 megabits per second (Mbit/s). USB 3.0 was released in 2008 is capable of maximum data transfer speeds up to 5 Gbit/s, which is 10 times faster than USB 2.0.

Many peripherals currently on the market still use the USB 2.0 standard, however, the newer USB 3.0 standard is steadily increasing in availability. If you purchase a device that uses the USB 3.0 standard, it's important to note that in order to take advantage of the added speed, all peripherals and cables within that chain have to be USB 3.0 compliant. So for example, if you purchase a hard drive that uses USB 3.0, then the cable, USB hub if any, and computer must also be USB 3.0 compatible to take advantage of the increased speed. However, USB 3.0 is backward compatible, so the devices will all work, but you will only experience speeds up to 480 Mbit/s.

Along with carrying data information, USB cables can also carry up to 5 volts of power. This is sufficient enough to power USB microphones, smaller audio interfaces, tablet computers, smart phones and other peripherals. Even MIDI keyboard controllers such as my M-Audio Oxygen 88 fully weighted keyboard is fully USB bus powered. Most desktops and laptops have USB slots that are bus-powered, allowing you to connect your device and receive power without the need of a separate power cord.

---

**TIP:**
When purchasing a USB hub, get one that features USB bus power and be sure to connect it to your wall outlet using the supplied power adapter. This will ensure that peripherals and devices connected to your hub will be able to receive the bus power.

---

## FireWire

Developed by Apple in the 1990s, the FireWire standard is also very common in home recording studios. FireWire comes in two standards, FireWire 400 (or IEEE 1394) that is more common and has a 6-pin connector, and FireWire 800 (IEEE 1394b) that has a 9-pin connector. FireWire 400 is capable data transfer speeds up to 400 Mbit/s, and FireWire 800 is capable of data transfer speeds up to 800 Mbit/s.

Like USB, FireWire also carries power along with data and can supply peripherals with up to 30 volts of power. A FireWire device can also be daisy-chained without the need of a hub, since it is a peer-to-peer based standard.

## USB vs. FireWire

While on paper USB 2.0 boasts a higher 480 Mbit/s transfer speed versus 400 Mbit/s for FireWire 400, FireWire is widely accepted as a faster standard. This is because in performance tests, FireWire has outperformed USB with higher "continuous" data transfer rates, versus the listed "maximum" rate. So for devices such as audio interfaces where audio data is continuously flowing through the cable, some music professionals prefer FireWire. Regarding audio interfaces in particular, the performance of current USB audio interfaces is comparable to FireWire audio interfaces. Through the years, product manufacturers have improved the quality of both the USB audio interface hardware and their corresponding software drivers.

The bottom line is that you should use the fastest standard you can for any particular device. For example, my audio interface uses USB 2.0, but I use FireWire 800 hard disk drives. My USB interface performs just as well, if not better, than any of my previous FireWire interfaces.

## MIDI

Musical Instrument Digital Interface (MIDI) was established in the early 1980s and is still the standard for connecting digital musical instruments. MIDI is used to facilitate communication between digital musical instruments and also with a computer. The original MIDI connection uses the DIN 5/180 degree connector. However, today MIDI information is widely carried using USB, FireWire and even Wi-Fi. Whereas using the 5-pin MIDI connector requires separate cables for MIDI in, out and through, these functions can be done using a single USB or FireWire cable, or with no cable using Wi-Fi.

## Analog Audio

The most common analog audio cables used in today's home recording studio include XLR balanced cables, TRS and TR cables, and RCA phono plugs.

**XLR** cables (or microphone cables) use a 3-pin connector and are balanced cables. An XLR cable is called "balanced" because it has three wires inside consisting of a hot line (positive), a cold line (negative) and earth (ground).

**TRS (tip, ring, sleeve)** connectors come in two popular sizes, the ¼" (6.35mm) and the 1/8" (3.5mm) miniature version. TRS connectors are commonly used as a balanced mono cable or an unbalanced stereo cable with both the left and right signals.

**FAQ:** When would I use a balanced TRS connector?

Use this when connecting balanced equipment such as mixers, audio interfaces, hardware effects processors and reference monitors. Also, some hardware synthesizers have balanced TRS connectors. As mentioned earlier, balanced cables will provide a stronger signal and lower noise so it's preferred in these cases.

**Balanced vs. Unbalanced**

Balanced cables provide a stronger audio signal and eliminate noise that is introduced to the cable by electricity, radio frequencies, etc. They eliminate noise by carrying both the audio signal and noise on the hot and cold lines, which are at opposite polarities. The audio signal is carried at opposite voltages, but the noise is not, so when the two lines are combined the noise cancels out.

**TR** cables also come in 1/4" and 1/8" versions. The TR cable is a mono unbalanced cable that is used as either a patch cable or for connecting electronic instruments such as an electronic guitar.

**RCA** connectors (or phono plugs) will be easily recognizable to anyone who works with consumer hi-fi equipment. Outside of hi-fi audio equipment, RCA connectors are still very popular on HD TV sets for connecting audio and analog video.

## Digital Audio

Digital audio cables have several advantages over analog cables. One obvious advantage is improved sound quality and wider audio bandwidth. Also, digital audio cables use digital code instead of electrical signals to carry sound, so they're less susceptible to picking up interference from electricity and radio signals in the air.

A variety of different digital cable formats are used to transport digital audio including: USB, FireWire, optical (TOSLINK) and coaxial (S/PDIF).

## Keeping it Neat

My wife teases me that I'm a bit of a "neat freak." I don't think I'm as bad as the TV character Monk, however, I do like every item to be in an aesthetically pleasing place and every cable to be out of sight. Keeping cables neat, orderly and out of sight is not only good for aesthetics, but it's also good to ensure they are not crossing electrical wires and picking up interference.

Here are some tips to help keep your cable lot neat and organized:

➤ **Keep cables tidy with Velcro.** For my home studio, I purchased industrial strength Velcro and Velcro One-Wraps (see Figure 3-21) that I picked up from a home goods store. I cut the industrial strength Velcro into one-inch squares and stuck the male side underneath my studio desk at different places. Then I used the Velcro One-Wrap ties to group runs of cables together and fastened them to the Velcro squares underneath the desk.

➤ **Label those cables.** Even a modest home recording studio can end up with a large amount of audio and data cables. Troubleshooting technical issues can be a challenge if you're not sure which cable is connected to the peripheral you're troubleshooting. Most office goods stores sell labels that can be marked appropriately and fastened to the ends of the cable.

➤ **Keep cable lengths as short as possible.** I mention this so often because it's that important. This is true of all cable types: analog, digital and electric. Using the shortest possible cable length needed for the job will minimize noise, enhance audio quality, reduce digital latency and help you keep a tidy recording space.

**Figure 3-20:** Velcro One-Wrap straps (left), and 2" Industrial Strength (right).

## Key Points from Chapter 3

- If you want maximum control of your music production software but have limited budget or desk space, then an "all-in-one" MIDI keyboard controller with faders, knobs and pads is a good investment.
- Get the best sound from your microphones by using high-quality cables, using a pop filter for recording vocals and placing the mic six to 12 inches from the sound source.
- Place your reference speakers so they create an equilateral triangle between each speaker and the listening position. Also monitor music at low volumes to avoid listening fatigue.
- Reduce latency with FireWire or USB audio interfaces by using short high-quality cables, optimizing your computer for audio recording and setting the lowest buffer size possible while recording.
- Use balanced cables to connect balanced audio equipment whenever possible.

# 4

# DIGITAL AUDIO WORKSTATION (DAW)

In This Chapter:

➢ What is a DAW?

➢ Which DAW is Right for You?

## What is a DAW?

The Digital Audio Workstation (DAW) is a computer-based music-recording platform that allows you to record and edit MIDI and audio with built-in virtual mixing, instruments and effects processors.

Back in the days, these functions were separated into different hardware devices. You first had to use traditional and electronic instruments to perform a musical idea that was recorded onto an analog or digital tape recorder. Then the completed recording was mixed using a hardware mixing console along with multiple hardware effects processors.

Today's DAWs provide all of this functionality in the box for thousands of dollars, if not hundreds of thousands, less.

## Which DAW is Right for You?

The DAW is the soul of your home recording studio. It has to flow with your way of thinking and become a tool to realize your ideas. It can't slow you down and must have basic features you'll need to create music.

In choosing the DAW that's right for you, you'll first need to ask yourself some questions:

- Do you plan to use a Mac or PC?
- Do you need music scoring?
- Are you looking for a very basic, easy-to-use platform that can be expanded later?
- Do you want maximum features from the start?
- Are you recording music that will be later worked on in commercial recording studios?
- Are you working on dance-oriented music? Rock? Jazz? Classical?
- Will you be recording a live band?

Once you better understand what you're looking for, you can more easily narrow down your choices.

## Popular Recording Software
While there are several DAWs on the market, many of which tout very similar features, several have become the more popular go-to DAWs and/or have established a niche.

Following are five popular DAWs on the market, and how they are best known:

## Pro Tools
Pro Tools (www.avid.com) is the industry standard DAW in commercial recording studios, and has been for some time. Its popularity in studios originated from it being an "audio recording" focused platform that had a graphic interface mimicking traditional recording hardware.

Pro Tools is a cross-platform (Mac and PC) DAW that comes in multiple versions, including a full version, a full HD version, and streamlined Express and SE versions that are included for free with popular audio interfaces.

While Pro Tools is still very popular in commercial recording studios, it is less popular with recording musicians since its MIDI editing and virtual instruments took some time to reach the level they are today. While the full version of Pro Tools is packed with MIDI editing, scoring and virtual instruments, in addition to its world-renowned audio editing, recording, mixing and virtual effects, it's still not as popular as a MIDI recording platform as it is an audio recording platform.

## Logic Pro

Logic Pro (www.apple.com) is the most popular DAW for the Mac. Produced by Apple, the same company that makes the computer and operating system, Logic is well known and respected by Mac users as a solid and dependable recording platform.

Logic Pro is a powerful Mac-only DAW with an array of virtual instruments, effects processors, audio and MIDI editing, and scoring. Logic previously had a smaller version named Express, however, that product has been discontinued, and its functionality was rolled into GarageBand. GarageBand comes bundled with every purchase of a Mac, and is a very powerful DAW comparable with commercially available entry-level DAWs.

While Logic is popular with Mac users, it has a reputation of being difficult to learn. Its MIDI editing is not the most intuitive and involves learning Logic's "environment." As a Mac user who owns Logic, I will say that learning Logic is very similar to learning all full-featured DAWs. It's an investment in time, but once mastered, becomes second nature.

## Cubase

Cubase (www.steinberg.net): Cubase is the most popular DAW on a PC, although it's a cross-platform DAW that's also very popular with Mac users. Cubase is known for having a workflow that is intuitive for musicians. Steinberg invented VST technology, the most popular standard for virtual instruments and effects, and was the first DAW to feature virtual instruments and effects built into recording software.

Cubase comes in three types, including its full-featured flagship version, a version called Artist, and a version called Elements. Artist and Elements feature the same graphic interface as the full version of Cubase, but each offers different levels of functionality from the complete package. While Elements is the entry-level DAW within the Cubase line, Steinberg also produces Sequel, an alternative entry-level DAW with a more basic and easy-to-use interface.

Similar to Logic, and all full-featured DAWs on this list, Cubase packs an enormous amount of features and will take an investment in time to learn and master. With that said, I own and use all of the DAWs on this list, but Cubase is the DAW that I use primarily. Years ago when I was searching for a DAW, I looked for a platform that would cater to my needs as a jazz musician wanting scoring and complete MIDI editing functionality. I found the workflow in Cubase to be the easiest and most intuitive to learn. However, the key reason it is still my go-to DAW is because I have invested years into learning all of its deepest secrets, and I've memorized a slew of key commands that make my workflow on Cubase speedy. This could just as easily be accomplished today using any of the other platforms mentioned.

## Ableton Live

Ableton Live (www.ableton.com) is a completely different DAW from the others. Its popularity comes from its focus as a live performance music platform, although it's also grown into a full-featured DAW. Ableton Live is not only used as a platform for live performance, but is also used as a performance instrument. It's very popular with DJs and producers who integrate Ableton Live with other music players such as turntables, to play music in clubs. Musicians and bands of all styles of music use Ableton Live to play prerecorded music during live performances.

Ableton Live is a cross-platform DAW that also has a scaled-down version named Ableton Live Intro. Intro uses the same interface as the full version and features most of the same functionality, but includes a limited amount of virtual instruments and effects. Ableton live does not feature music scoring.

Many users of other DAW packages also use Ableton Live. Outside of the live environment, Ableton Live is often used as a "scratchpad" for recording ideas quickly using its highly intuitive pattern-based Session View. These ideas can later be recorded into a linear-based DAW for mix-down, or recorded and mixed using Ableton Live's Arrangement View. The pattern-based way of working has a loyal following, and is often preferred by producers of urban, dance and electronic music genres.

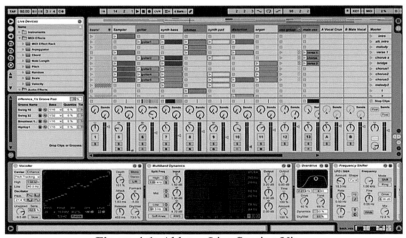

**Figure 4-1:** Ableton Live Session View.

## Reason

Reason (www.propellerheads.se) is another popular DAW with a niche following that packs a lot of features. Until recently, Reason was not a DAW at all. It became popular as a virtual studio rack of instruments and effects that could easily be stacked into creative and inspiring configurations. Its interface was known for mimicking traditional studio racks, and it enabled you to flip the rack around and patch any instrument or effect to any other. It had MIDI sequencing that could be used to capture ideas, and then you could use ReWire to patch audio from Reason into your DAW of choice to record and mix audio tracks.

Today Reason is still promoted as a virtual studio rack, but it also features a complete virtual mixing console, as well as audio and MIDI recording and editing. While Reason now has audio recording and editing capability, this functionality is a fairly recent addition and doesn't yet match the level of capability found in Pro Tools, Logic or Cubase.

Reason comes in two versions, including the full-featured version and Reason Essentials. Reason Essentials has the same interface and MIDI functionality as the full version, but has a scaled back mixer and limited virtual instruments and effects. Reason does not feature music scoring.

> ❖ For a complete listing of popular DAWs including Sonar, Digital Performer and FL Studio, visit http://www.homemusicproduction.com/music-recording-and-production-software-daw-roundup/.

## Key Points from Chapter 4

- Most DAWS today have similar functionality, but feature different graphic interfaces and workflows.
- In choosing a DAW, consider your needs and preferred method of working. Download software demos when possible to test its workflow.
- Different DAWs are popular for different reasons. Don't choose a DAW simply because it's what everyone else uses... unless you plan on mixing your tracks in several commercial studios.

# VIRTUAL INSTRUMENTS AND EFFECTS

## In This Chapter:

➢ DAW Plug-in Formats

➢ Jack of All Trades vs. Master of One

➢ Virtual Instruments

➢ Virtual Effects

## DAW Plug-in Formats

Most DAWs come with a variety of virtual instruments and effects. All of the five DAWs listed in Chapter 4 come complete with: samplers, drum machines, synthesizers, EQ, compressors, delays and a whole lot more. For almost all recording situations, these instruments and effects will provide you with a sufficient palette of sounds and possibilities to compose, record, mix and master music.

DAW developers also allow third-party developers to create software plug-ins that can expand the DAW's sound palate even further. Virtual instrument and effects plug-ins come in different formats designed to work with the various proprietary DAW platforms.

Some of the popular plug-in formats include:

- VST
- RTAS
- AU
- ReWire
- Rack Extension

# VST

The VST (Virtual Studio Technology) format is the most popular and widely used plug-in format. You may also see it listed as VSTi, in which the "i" stands for "instrument" to differentiate the instrument plug-ins from the effects.

The VST plug-in format was launched by Steinberg in 1996 and was the first instrument and effects plug-in platform invented. It was released as an open universal format, so other software developers could also create plug-ins using this format. Not all DAW developers adopted the VST format and some such as Digidesign (now Avid), Apple and Cakewalk decided to create their own plug-in formats.

Steinberg continues to update the VST format, and with version 3 (VST3) introduced features such as Note Expression (which allows articulation control per note instead of per MIDI channel), and improved performance by applying processing only when audio signals are present.

VST plug-ins will work in mostly all DAWs with the exception of Logic (AU), Pro Tools (RTAS) and Reason (Rack Extension).

# RTAS

Digidesign (now Avid) developed the RTAS (Real-Time AudioSuite) plug-in format for its Pro Tools music production platform. RTAS plug-ins will work with all versions of Pro Tools, but are not natively compatible with any other DAW platform.

Most third-party developers that create RTAS plug-ins also create VST versions of the same plug-in. However, the reverse is not always true. Third-party VST developers may not always create RTAS versions of a plug-in. Thankfully, FXpansion (www.fxpansion.com) produces VST to RTAS Adapter. This software will wrap your VST plug-ins and ready them for use in any version of Pro Tools.

# AU

Apple Computer developed the AU (Audio Units) plug-in format. AU plug-ins work with Apple's Logic Pro and Garage Band.

Similar to the RTAS format, not all VST plug-ins are available in the AU format. FXpansion also produces VST to AU Adapter, which will allow you to use any VST plug-in within Logic or Garage Band.

## ReWire

ReWire is not a plug-in format, but is a software protocol that streams music from one application to another. Jointly developed by Steinberg and Propellerhead, ReWire lets you add mixer tracks in your DAW and stream in stereo or individual tracks from another ReWire enabled software platform.

For example, you can use ReWire to stream audio tracks from Ableton Live or Reason into Cubase, Pro Tools or Logic.

## Rack Extension

Created by Propellerhead in 2012, Rack Extension is the newest plug-in format of the bunch. Rack Extension is a plug-in format that only works inside of Reason's Virtual Studio Racks. Before the release of Rack Extension, Reason software did not allow any third-party plug-ins.

> **TIP:**
> It's important to note that not all third party VST and RTAS plug-ins work cross-platform on both Mac and PC. Double-check before purchasing any plug-in that is compatible with your computer platform.

# Jack of All Trades vs. Master of One

Virtual instrument and effect plug-ins tend to fall into one of two categories: the jack of all trades and the master of one.

When you decide to enhance your DAW's capabilities and sound palette with additional third-party plug-ins, you'll need to consider the role the plug-in will play in your music.

Ask yourself:

- ✓ Do you need to cover a lot of ground with one purchase?

- ✓ Do you need to replicate an instrument or effect to the finest detail, or simply acquire a sound that is close enough?

Some plug-ins cover as much ground as possible by offering a wide variety of instruments or effects in one package. An example of this type of instrument plug-in is Kontakt by Native Instruments (www.native-instruments.com). Kontakt, and in fact most virtual samplers, typically provide a wide range of sounds emulating acoustic instruments from pianos, strings and orchestral sounds, to synths, drums and world instrument sounds. These software packages often come with multiple gigabytes of samples to cover hundreds or thousands of sound presets.

Dedicated virtual instruments may also come with gigabytes of samples, however, they cover only one type of instrument. For example, Trilian virtual bass instrument by Spectrasonics (www.spectrasonics.net) comes with a 34GB library of sounds dedicated solely to bass instruments.

**So which one is right for you?** If your goal is composing music that will later be re-recorded by musicians, then the sound library provided for free with your DAW or the sound library bundled with Kontakt will do fine. If you intend to record and publish acoustic-sounding music using only virtual instruments (as I do), then you will at some point want to build a collection of dedicated virtual instruments. However, your focus should be acquiring only the instruments that are key to the type of music you are producing. Try to keep your computer system uncluttered and free of unnecessary plug-ins.

Since I record piano-focused music, having a powerful and realistic virtual piano is essential. The three virtual pianos that I use consistently are The Grand 3 by Steinberg (www.steinberg.net), Ivory II Grand Pianos by Synthogy (www.synthogy.com) and Vintage D Virtual Grand by Galaxy Instruments (www.galaxypianos.com). Each of these instruments contains many gigabytes of samples and captures just about every nuance of an acoustic piano. Also, these virtual piano instruments have unique qualities that are different from each other so I choose them for compositions as selectively as if I were choosing a Steinway piano versus a Yamaha Piano.

When it comes to effects plug-ins, good examples of "all-in-one" plug-ins are Guitar Rig by Native Instruments and MAGMA Virtual Studio Rack by Nomad Factory ([www.nomadfactory.com](http://www.nomadfactory.com)).  Guitar Rig was initially developed as a guitar amp emulation package, but has since evolved into a full virtual effects rack.  MAGMA Virtual Studio Rack has 65 unique effects covering a range of effects like reverb, delay, EQ and tape emulation, just to name a few.  Both Guitar Rig and MAGMA allow you to instantiate only one plug-in, yet have access to a multitude of effects.

By contrast, dedicated effects plug-ins perform only one function. When you're just starting out producing music at home, I recommend holding off on these types of third-party plug-ins until you get proficient at recording and mixing music in your DAW and have a better understanding of what specific needs you may have.  New home studio often producers purchase too many "must have" effects plug-ins, and then feel obligated to use them all on recorded tracks.  The resulting mix can end up being overly processed with effects that may not be necessary to make the music sound great.

## The Channel Strip
A recent category of multi-effects plug-ins is the virtual channel strip.  They emulate the channel strips found on traditional hardware mixers where the sound travels from the mixer input through compression, EQ and limiter modules.

Examples of virtual channel strips include:

- iZotope Alloy 2 ([www.izotope.com](http://www.izotope.com))
- Waves SSL G-Channel ([www.waves.com](http://www.waves.com))
- Solid State Logic Duende Native Channel Strip ([www.solid-state-logic.com](http://www.solid-state-logic.com))
- Waves Arts TrackPlug ([www.wavearts.com](http://www.wavearts.com))
- Team DNR MixControl Pro ([www.teamdnr.net](http://www.teamdnr.net))

All of these virtual channel strips provide a chain of dynamics effects that are available in one instance of the plug-in.  One of the benefits of channel strip plug-ins is the pure convenience of having essential effects all in one place.

I happen to be a fan of Alloy 2 by iZotope.  It includes all of the essential dynamics effects, including a compressor, limiter, de-esser, and EQ with spectrum analyzer available in one instance of the plug-in.  It's light on your computer's processor and only uses system resources for the specific effects that are activated.  Lastly, it's got digital and vintage emulations to cater to just about every sound you may be looking to create.  At $149, it's a high-quality channel strip at an affordable price.

# Virtual Instruments

With a wealth of virtual instruments on the market, everyone will have his or her own favorite virtual synth and drum machine based on personal taste and musical preferences. In this section, I'll provide you with a good understanding of the various types of virtual instruments that exist as well as some product examples.

At the end of this chapter, I provide a link to a listing of the virtual instruments and effects software I'm currently using in my home studio to create music. This will give you some ideas of specific software that can be used for specific instrumentation needs.

I separate the various types of virtual instruments into four categories:

1) Virtual Samplers
2) Modeled Instruments
3) Virtual Synths
4) Virtual Drums

## Virtual Samplers

Virtual Samplers enable you to play back audio recordings using a MIDI controller. Oddly enough, most of the popular virtual samplers on the market don't have the one feature that their hardware counterparts had as a standard. They don't actually enable you to record (or sample) directly into the plug-in. Instead they often use a drag-and-drop method to get prerecorded audio files into the virtual sampler software.

Sample players are similar to samplers in that they play libraries of sampled virtual instruments, however, they only play back preset sounds and don't allow you to import your own audio recordings.

Some developers of sample libraries start out creating sample libraries for established samplers, such as NI's Kontakt, then later develop their own proprietary sample playback engine and sell the sample library as a complete dedicated instrument. A good example of this are sample libraries by East West such as RA, which started as a library available for Kontakt before being moved to East West's own PLAY sample player engine.

Here are some popular free sample players that are "player-only" versions of larger sampling software packages:

- **Kontakt Player** (www.native-instruments.com) is a free version of Native Instruments' flagship Kontakt sampler. Kontakt Player is a free download from NI's website and provides 50 instruments and 500 MB of sample content.

- **Independence FREE** (www.pro.magix.com) is the free version of Independence PRO, the powerful sampler by Magix. Independence FREE comes with a whopping 2.5GB of premium instruments selected from the Independence PRO library.

Here's a listing of full-functioning samplers that come bundled with popular DAWs:

- **ESX24** sampler is bundled with Apple's Logic Pro.

- **NN-XT** sampler is bundled with Propellerhead's Reason.

- **Simpler** sampler is bundled with the standard versions of Ableton Live. **Sampler** is bundled with the larger Ableton Suite package, and is also sold separately for those who purchase standard versions of Ableton Live.

Both Pro Tools and Cubase include free sample players that are scaled-down versions of their flagship samplers, which are sold separately.

## Modeled Instruments

Modeled instruments use complex algorithms and programming to create physically modeled emulations of acoustic and analog instruments. Virtual instruments that use physical modeling are designed to emulate the intricate nuances and behavior of an instrument that may only be possible via samplers using large amounts of samples and complex scripting. Modeled instruments may use synthesis techniques only or a combination of sampling and synthesis techniques. Modeled instruments offer realistic sound, require little RAM and sometimes provide less strain on your CPU.

**Figure 5-1:** HALion 4 sampler by Steinberg. HALion 4 is a complete sampler with a built-in synthesis engine. Cubase bundles with HALion Sonic SE, a sample player version of HALion 4.

**Figure 5-2:** Ms. Sax S. modeled soprano saxophone by Sample Modeling.

Here are a couple of developers who specialize in creating modeled instruments:

- **Sample Modeling** (www.samplemodeling.com) develops modeled brass and woodwind instruments that use both sampling and complex algorithms to emulate sounds. These instruments lend themselves very well to MIDI wind controllers.

- **PianoTeq** (www.pianoteq.com) by Modartt is a good example of physically modeled instruments without the use of samples. PianoTeq emulates several types of acoustic pianos, electric pianos and mallet instruments.


## Virtual Synths

Virtual synths are instruments that can reproduce sound using a variety of synthesis methods. While the purpose of sampled and modeled instruments is to emulate acoustic instruments as closely as possible, the main purpose of synthesizers is to create new and original sounds that may or may not resemble an acoustic instrument.

Virtual synthesizers are typically classified as either analog or digital sounding instruments. This stems from the legacy hardware instruments of the past that either used analog circuitry or digital processors to recreate sound. All of today's virtual instruments are digital, so a reference to either analog or digital is merely a descriptive reference of the type of sound it produces.

Here are four popular synthesis methods used today, all of which can be used to create rich sonic textures:

1) **Subtractive Synthesis** creates timbre by using filters to cut away (or subtract) parts of the harmonics you don't want to hear. This is the most popular synthesis method used for hardware and software analog synths.

2) **Frequency Modulation** (or FM) synthesis creates timbre by using a sine wave oscillator as a carrier wave, and using another oscillator as a modulating wave. This is also known as Phase Modulation. It was the method used by the popular Yamaha DX-7 synth of the '80s, and is the synthesis method used by Native Instruments' FM8 virtual synth today.

3) **Granular Synthesis** recreates sound by taking sampled waveforms and chopping them up into small slices 1 to 50ms called grains. This method of synthesizing sounds is gaining in popularity, and is used in Padshop and Padshop Pro virtual synthesizers by Steinberg (www.steinberg.net).

4) **Hybrid Synthesizers** isn't a specific type of synthesis, however, this term is widely used to describe synthesizers that employ multiple synthesis methods.

One type of hybrid synth is sample-based synths that use sampled waveforms instead of, or in addition to, fundamental waveforms to create sounds. An example of this type of hybrid synth is Omnisphere by Spectrasonics (www.spectrasonics.net).

Another type of hybrid synth is one that employs multiple types of synthesis methods. A good example of this is Electra X by Tone 2 (www.tone2.com). Electra X has 13 different synth methods that can be used alone and combined to create rich sonic textures.

---

**TIP:** The best way to learn basic synthesis programming is to use a simple two-oscillator analogue-type synth (free with most DAWs), and manipulate the various oscillators, envelopes and filters until you become familiar with what they do and how they work.

---

## Virtual Drums

Virtual drums are designed to emulate either acoustic drums and drumming techniques, or the classic drum machines of the past. The virtual drum instrument that is right for you will largely depend on the style of music you're creating, and the manner in which you like programming drums.

One method of programming drum tracks is to load up a virtual drum instrument and record sequences in real-rime to your DAW using a MIDI controller. Another method of drum programming is to use a virtual drum machine or groove machine to sequence rhythm patterns, and sync the patterns to your DAW.

Virtual drum instruments come in four flavors:

1) Sampled Drum Players
2) Virtual Drum Synths
3) Groove Machines
4) Virtual Drummers

## Sampled Drum Players

This is the most common virtual drum instrument and is typically bundled with all popular DAWs on the market. A sample drum player is a virtual instrument that comes with a collection of sampled drum sounds and will often allow you to drag in your own drum samples. **Battery 3** by Native Instruments is good example of a commercially available sampled drum player.

This category also includes dedicated sampled acoustic drum instruments. These are drum instruments geared toward providing the most accurate emulation of an acoustic drum kit. These instruments typically do not allow you to use your own samples.

Examples of popular dedicated sampled acoustic drum instruments include:

- **EZdrummer** and **Superior Drummer 2.0** by Toontrack (www.toontrack.com)
- **Addictive Drums** by XLN Audio (www.xlnaudio.com)
- **Steven Slate Drums** (www.stevenslatedrums.com)
- **BFD2** by FXpansion (www.fxpansion.com)

All of the aforementioned sampled drum instruments specialize in producing natural-sounding acoustic drum kits along with the ambience of the recorded space. They include MIDI grooves performed by actual drummers that you can use in your music to provide realistic drum rhythms. They also offer expansion drum kits sold separately that offer alternative drum kits, including electronic and drum machine sampled drum sounds.

**Figure 5-3:** EZdrummer sample drum player by Toontrack.

## Virtual Drum Synths

This category emulates drum sounds of analog hardware drum synths of the past such as the legendary Roland TR-808 drum machine. Virtual drum synths use synthesis and physical modeling instead of sampling to generate drum sounds.

Most products within this category are referred to as virtual drum machines, and include a rhythm sequencer similar to the sequencers found on the hardware drum machines they emulate.

Here are a couple of virtual drum synths by developers who specialize in creating modeled drum synth instruments:

- **SPARK Vintage** by Arturia (www.arturia.com) uses synthesis, physical modeling, and some sampling to recreate 30 classic drum machines.

  Arturia also produces SPARK Creative Drum Machine, which is a hardware and software hybrid drum machine. SPARK comes with 90 drum kits, including the 30 kits from SPARK Vintage.

- **ADM AudioRealism Drum Machine** by AudioRealism (www.audiorealism.se) uses physical modeling to recreate three classic drum machines (Rolands TR-606, TR-808, and TR-909).

## Groove Machines

Groove machines are widely popular with producers of urban, dance and electronic music genres. This category of drum instrument became popular in the '90s with the Akai MPC hardware series of groove samplers.

While drum machines focus on having a set of internal drum sounds and include a rhythm sequencer to record patterns and songs, groove machines include those features and add sampling, loop playing, loop slicing, time stretching and, in some cases, host other VST and AU instruments. Groove machines are viewed as complete music production solutions with an emphasis on groove production.

Here are three popular virtual groove machines currently on the market:

1) **Geist** by FXpansion (www.fxpansion.com) is a virtual sampler and groove machine that features true sampling directly within the software either in plug-in or stand-alone mode. Geist is compatible with any MIDI controller.

2) **Maschine** by Native Instruments (www.native-instruments.com) is a hardware and software hybrid groove machine that features near total control of the software using the Maschine hardware.

3) **MPC Renaissance** by Akai (www.akaiprompc.com) is a hardware and software hybrid groove machine that follows the tradition of the classic Akai MPC series. The hardware offers complete tactile control of the software.

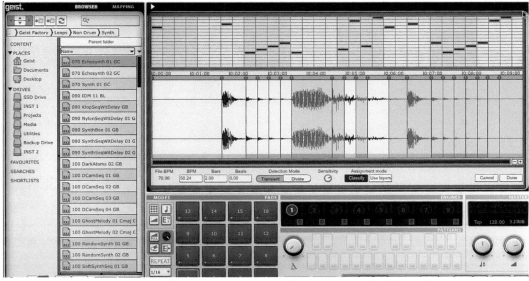

**Figure 5-4:** Geist sample groove and drum machine by FXpansion.

## Virtual Drummers

Like sampled virtual drums, virtual drumming instruments are designed to provide very realistic and natural sounding drum kits. What makes these instruments unique is how they generate drum rhythms. Instead of providing libraries of rhythm MIDI files, they include rhythm generators that use programming and algorithms to simulate drummer-playing styles.

Virtual drummers are great if you work in genres that require natural-sounding live drums such as singer-songwriter, country, pop, rock and jazz styles. They work by providing you with a selection of options that offer different styles and playing intensities.

There aren't many virtual drummer products on the market, but here are a few good ones:

- **MDrummer** by MeldaProduction (www.meldaproduction.com) is a complete virtual drummer with plenty of great features. It works on both PC and OS X platforms and comes with a 6GB library of acoustic and electronic drum sounds.

- **Jamstix** by Rayzoon (www.rayzoon.com) works on PCs only at the current time, however, an OS X version is in the works. It comes with a 1.3GB library of drum sounds and allows VST sub-hosting, so you can use drum sounds from existing products such as EZ Drummer, Addictive Drums, etc.

- **Strike** by Avid (www.avid.com) works only with Pro Tools on both PC and OS X systems. It comes with a 30GB library of drum sounds and a very easy-to-use interface.

# Virtual Effects

As I mentioned earlier in this chapter, I recommend using the virtual effects that come bundled with your DAW when you're first setting up and learning your home recording studio. Become familiar and proficient with these tools first before considering any third-party effects plug-ins. Your DAW's effects plug-ins will be native to the DAW's environment and will maximize the efficiency of your DAW and CPU.

Here are my two exceptions to this rule:

✓ **Guitar amp emulation software.** If you're a guitarist, then getting the perfect guitar tone is essential to crafting your signature sound. Amp emulation software that comes with today's DAWs is simply not on the same level as such plug-ins by third-party developers who have spent years developing their amp emulations software. Further along in this chapter I discuss Amp Emulation Software in more depth.

✓ **EQ with built-in spectrum analyzer.** I prefer to use an EQ that has a built-in spectrum analyzer. Most monitor speakers used in a home studio have a 5" woofer and a low frequency range of 50 Hz. When listening to your track with such speakers, there may be low energy below 50 Hz that you simply can't hear and are therefore unaware of. A spectrum analyzer is a great tool to help you identify those frequencies and treat them appropriately.

A few DAWs such as Logic come with an EQ that has an integrated spectrum analyzer, however, Cubase does not, so I use the EQ within Alloy 2 when I need a more visual equalizer for "surgical" EQ.

A couple of really good spectrum analyzers without EQ that are also free are:

• **SPAN** by Voxengo (www.voxengo.com)
• **FreqAnalyst** by Blue Cat Audio (www.bluecataudio.com)


## Processors and Effects

While I broadly use the terms "Virtual Effects" or "Virtual Effect Processors," I have to point out that *technically* processors and effects are not actually the same.

A processor – such as an equalizer, compressor, limiter or gate - is typically placed as an insert in your DAW mixer and is used to treat and replace the original signal with a new processed signal.

An effect – such as a reverb, delay, chorus or flanger – is typically placed on a "send" channel in addition to the original signal.

With that said, that fact is purely a matter of semantics since both effects and processors are used as effects to enhance music tracks in fresh and unique ways.

**Figure 5-5:** Alloy 2 channel strip plug-in by iZotope. This multi-effect plug-in contains essential dynamics processors including: EQ, transient, exciter, two compressors, de-esser and a limiter.

Here are the essential processors and effects used to create professional-sounding recordings and mixes:

## Equalizers

EQ is arguably the single most important signal processor in mixing after the fader and panner. An EQ is simply a volume control for specific frequencies within a sound. Most DAWs have two types of EQ plug-ins available: parametric and graphic.

Parametric EQ is the one most commonly used in a DAW. It allows complete flexibility to pinpoint the exact frequencies you want to boost or attenuate, and also allows control of the width of the frequency band.

Graphic EQs have a set of fixed filter bands. The more of these bands a graphic EQ has, the tighter the width of the band will be. So the filters on a 31-band graphic EQ will have a narrower bandwidth than the filters on a 10-band graphic EQ.

## Compressors

A compressor controls the volume of peaks within a sound. After EQ, a compressor is the second most important processor in mixing. Using a compressor is like having your hand on the volume fader and turning down the volume when the sound gets too loud, then increasing the volume back to its original position when the sound returns to normal.

Compressors can be used on individual tracks or on an entire mix and should be applied sparingly. Overuse of compression creates an obvious loud again, soft again effect known as pumping, and can make the track sound artificially or overly squashed.

## Expanders

An expander is essentially a compressor in reverse. Instead of decreasing the volume during peaks in the audio, an expander increases the volume of sound when it drops below a certain threshold.

An expander can also work by decreasing the volume of quiet portions of the sound, thus expanding the distance between the loud and soft passages. The most common application for this is to reduce background noise in a microphone. An expander can be set to kick in and reduce the volume when the sound gets below a set threshold.

## Gates

A gate does the same thing as an Expander, but to the extreme. Instead of simply turning down the volume during softer passages, it closes the gates completely and shuts off the sound once the signal gets below a set threshold.

Gates are commonly used on live drum and percussion sounds to "clean up" or "tighten" the sound of the drum. In the '80s, gates were commonly used in an effects chain after a reverb effect to quickly shut off a highly reverberated drum sound (think Phil Collins).

## Limiters

A limiter works in the same way as a compressor, but instead of reducing the volume by a certain ratio, it ensures that absolutely no sound gets above a predetermined level. This is commonly referred to as "brick wall" limiting.

Used on individual tracks or an entire mix, limiters are commonly set to 0.0 dB or below to prevent a signal from clipping or distorting.

## Reverbs

Reverb effects are used to create space for a specific track, or to give an entire mix a common overall ambience.

Natural reverb is created when sound is produced in a room and bounces off the walls, creating a large number of tiny echoes that decay as the sound is slowly absorbed. A reverb plug-in recreates this effect digitally.

Convolution reverb is also a digitally created reverb. However, instead of using programmed algorithms to emulate the sound of various reverberated spaces, convolution reverbs use recorded samples of real rooms to model and simulate a specific space. Convolution reverbs are touted as sounding more natural than standard digital reverbs, but are very taxing on CPU.

## Digital Delays

A delay effect takes an audio signal and plays it back after a predetermined period of time. A delay effect can be programmed to repeat the source sound only once, or multiple times like fading echoes.

Like reverbs, delays are used to give an instrument or vocal track the illusion of space. Delays can be used in place of, or in addition to reverbs to create a natural sounding ambience.

Delay and reverb effects should be applied sparingly to prevent the track or overall mix from sounding muddy and washed out.

## Chorus

Chorus effect provides a layered sound, making an instrument or voice sound like a group of instruments or voices. It works by doubling and delaying the sound and altering the pitch slightly.

Chorus is commonly used on guitars, pad sounds, electric pianos and sometimes vocals for added depth and warmth.

## Amp Emulation Software

Amp emulation software digitally reproduces classic hardware guitar amp, microphone and stomp pedal effects chains. With the quality of amp emulation software making it next to impossible to differentiate between modeled amps and the real thing, more guitarists are choosing to ditch their expensive amp setups and are opting to create their killer tones in the box.

Popular DAWs such as Pro Tools, Cubase, Logic and Ableton Live all feature amp emulation software as part of their effects suite. If you're looking for more than the amp emulation software that comes bundled with your DAW, here are some popular options to check out:

- **AmpliTube** (www.ikmultimedia.com): AmpliTube was first released in 2002, making it one of the first guitar amp emulation and effects software on the market. IK Multimedia now develops a suite of amp modeling software including Fender, Jimi Hendrix, Metal and Ampeg (bass) versions of AmpliTube.

- **Guitar Rig Pro** (www.native-instruments.com): Guitar Rig was first released in 2004, and is also a well-established amp emulation software package. Since its release, Guitar Rig has expanded beyond amp emulation and now also features more than 50 high-quality digital effects.

- **ReValver** (www.peavey.com): Having been in the guitar amp making business since 1965, Peavey knows a thing or two about guitar amps. ReValver is Peavey's entry into the amp emulation fray, and it boasts a very robust feature set of modeled amps, speaker cabinets, microphones, stomp boxes and digital effects.

- **POD Farm** (www.line6.com): POD Farm by Line 6 has a very full set of features, amp models and digital effects to choose from. Line 6 also develops stomp pedalboard controllers that work with the POD Farm stomp boxes and effects.

- **GTR** (www.wavesgtr.com): Waves is no small player in the world of high-quality digital effects plug-ins. Modeled after amps by well-known manufacturers such as Marshall, Ibanez and Carvin, GTR features a healthy set of amps, speaker cabinets, stomp boxes and microphones.

**Figure 5-6:** Pod Farm 2.5 amp emulation software by Line 6.

❖ Visit http://www.homemusicproduction.com/guitar-interface-and-amp-emulation-software-round-up for the latest information on guitar interfaces and amp emulation software.

❖ Visit http://www.homemusicproduction.com/studiotour2 to see a current listing of the virtual instruments and effects I'm using in my home studio to create music.

## Key Points from Chapter 5

- Decide if an all-in-one virtual instrument or effect is right for your needs, or if you prefer one plug-in dedicated to a specific task.
- Use and master your DAWs virtual effects plug-ins FIRST before looking into third-party virtual effects.
- Consider using a spectrum analyzer, or an EQ with spectrum analyzer to assist you in identifying and correcting sound frequencies.
- The most popular and most expensive virtual effects plug-ins available will NOT make your music sound any better than the effects that are bundled with your DAW.
- The most popular and most expensive virtual instrument in history, on its own, has never made a hit record.

# GOING MOBILE

## In This Chapter:

➤ Using an iPad for Music Production

➤ Mobile DAW Apps

➤ Synthesizer and Groove Apps

➤ Connecting an iPad to Your DAW

## Using an iPad for Music Production

In the section in Chapter 3 on "Using an iPad as a Controller," I listed some of the applications available for the iPad that can be used to control your DAW and software plug-ins.   Now let's look at some other ways an iPad can be integrated with your music production setup and workflow.

How is the iPad being used for music production in the real world?

- ✓ As a primary self-contained music recording workstation
- ✓ As a music-composing sketchpad to capture ideas while away from the studio
- ✓ To play prerecorded tracks during live performance
- ✓ For guitar amp and effects tones during live performance and in the studio
- ✓ As a dedicated synth, drum and sampler instrument
- ✓ As a remote controller for computer-based applications (using controller apps listed in Chapter 3)

**Outside of Music Production**

I also use the iPad extensively to capture and organize my thoughts and ideas. Using Evernote's (www.evernote.com) note-taking app, I capture many ideas including potential song and album titles, music production notes, recording to-do lists, plans for future projects and so much more. With Evernote's audio recording function, I even use it to record my hummed melodies when I'm away from my setup and inspiration strikes.

# Mobile DAW Apps

Mobile DAW apps have come a long way since the iPad was released in 2010. The current crop of mobile DAW apps for iPad is very usable for either capturing music ideas quickly while you're on the road, or as your primary means of recording music.

Here are five very good mobile DAW apps for the iPad (all of which are 100 times more powerful than the Tascam 234 4-track recorder I used when I started recording music):

- **GarageBand** by Apple (www.apple.com)

- **FL Studio Mobile HD** by Image Line Software (www.image-line.com)

- **Music Studio** by Xewton (www.xewton.com)

- **Beatmaker 2** by Intua (www.intua.net)

- **iSequence** by BeepStreet (www.beepstreet.com)

**Figure 6-1:** Music Studio digital audio workstation for iPad by Xewton.

❖ Visit http://www.homemusicproduction.com/ipad-daw-app-comparison/ for a current listing and detailed comparison of these top mobile music workstations for iPad.

# Synthesizer and Groove Apps

There is a wealth of synthesizer and groove production apps available for the iPad. Unfortunately, many sound like toys and are not suitable for professional music production. There are, however, some very good sounding synth and groove apps for iPad that have rich sounds and great features.

Here some popular and professional-sounding synth and groove apps available for the iPad:

- **Sunrizer Synth** by BeepStreet (www.beepstreet.com) is a virtual analog synth for iPad that features rich analog sound, effects and an arpeggiator.

- **IMS-20** by Korg (www.korg.com) is a complete recreation of Korg's MS-20 hardware synth. It also includes a drum machine and 16-step analog sequencer.

- **Animoog** by Moog (www.moogmusic.com) is an analog-sounding synth designed for the iPad that recreates a variety of classic Moog analog synth sounds.

- **Alchemy Mobile** by Camel Audio (www.camelaudio.com) is an iPad version of Camel Audio's powerful computer-based Alchemy synth. The app features a multi-synthesis engine, an arpeggiator, and is also a wireless remote controller for the computer-based Alchemy synth.

- **iElectribe** by Korg is an iPad version of Korg's hardware Electribe R drum machine. It features analog synth drums, effects and a rhythm sequencer.

- **Molten Drum Machine** by On Red Dog (www.onereddog.com.au) is a synth and sample drum machine used to create percussive sounds and rhythm sequences.

- **ReBirth for iPad** by Propellerhead (www.propellerheads.se) is an iPad version of Propellerhead's discontinued ReBirth computer-based software synth. It emulates the sounds of the Roland TR-303 Bass Synth, and the Roland TR-808 and 909 drum machines.

**Figure 6-2:** Sunrizer synth for iPad by BeepStreet (left). Alchemy Mobile synth for iPad by Camel Audio (right).

❖ Visit http://www.homemusicproduction.com/using-your-ipad-as-an-external-midi-synth-or-drum-machine/ for additional information on music apps and iPad connection options.

# Connecting an iPad to Your Studio

Depending on the intended use, there are a few different ways to connect your iPad to your studio gear.

Here are some practical scenarios:

- You want to play and record music into an iPad music app using a MIDI controller.

- You want to plug an electric guitar, bass or microphone into the iPad and record its audio.

- You want to use an iPad synth or groove app as an external sound source and record it into your computer-based DAW.

- You want to use the iPad to wirelessly control your computer-based DAW and plug-ins.

Now let's take a look at some of the methods used to connect your iPad to your home studio gear:

## Method 1: iPad Camera Connection Kit

If you want to play and record music into an iPad music app using a MIDI input device such as a MIDI keyboard controller, you can easily achieve this with an iPad Camera Connection Kit by Apple (www.apple.com). With an iPad camera connection kit and a standard USB cable, you can connect any USB class compliant MIDI keyboard controller directly into the iPad.

A class compliant USB device (also known as "plug and play") refers to any USB device that doesn't require third-party software drivers. Many of today's MIDI controllers are class compliant, but confirm this on the manufacturer's website before attempting to connect a MIDI controller to your iPad.

**Figure 6-3:** iPad Camera Connection Kit adapter by Apple.

## Method 2: iPad Audio and MIDI Interfaces

If you want to plug an electric guitar, bass or microphone into the iPad and record its audio, then an iPad audio interface is needed. If you want your computer-based DAW to control an iPad synthesizer or drum groove app via MIDI, then an iPad MIDI interface is needed.

Here are some examples of both:

- **iConnectMIDI** by iConnectivity (www.iconnectivity.com) is a complete MIDI interface solution that allows 5-pin MIDI, USB MIDI, Mac, PC and iOS devices to all connect at the same time.

- **MIDI Mobilizer** by Line 6 (www.line6.com) is a MIDI interface for iPad with 5-pin MIDI input and output connectors.

- **iRig** by IK Multimedia ([www.ikmultimedia.com](www.ikmultimedia.com)) is an audio interface for iPad that allows you to plug in an electric guitar or bass and record its audio into an iPad music app. IK Multimedia has a collection of iRig products to connect microphones, MIDI and other devices to the iPad.

- **iXZ** by Tascam ([www.tascam.com](www.tascam.com)) is an audio interface for iPad with an XLR and ¼" input, microphone preamp and phantom power.

**Figure 6-4:** iConnectMIDI multi-device MIDI interface by iConnectivity.

## Method 3: iPad Studio Docking Stations:

iPad studio docking stations combine both audio and MIDI interfaces in one unit that also keeps your iPad charged. This would be an ideal solution if you intend to keep the iPad in your home studio and want to leave the MIDI and audio cables connected.

Here are two popular iPad studio docking stations with both MIDI and audio connectivity:

- **iO Dock** by Alesis ([www.alesis.com](www.alesis.com))
- **Studio Connect** by Griffen ([www.griffintechnology.com](www.griffintechnology.com))

## Method 4: iPad Wireless connection via Wi-Fi

In Chapter 3, I discussed apps that enable you to use the iPad to control your computer-based DAW and other software. These apps can communicate with your computer via a standard MIDI connection using an iO Dock or iConnectMIDI, or they can communicate with your computer via Wi-Fi.

Each controller app uses proprietary intermediate software that allows the iPad and computer to communicate. They also require a virtual MIDI port, so the DAW knows where to assign the incoming MIDI channel.

Mac computers use CoreMIDI, which is built into OS X to establish virtual MIDI ports. PCs require third-party software such as **LoopMIDI** (www.tobias-erichsen.de/software/loopmidi.html) or **MIDI Yoke** (www.midiox.com).

## Connecting Your iPad and Computer via Wi-Fi

If you plan to use apps that wirelessly connect the iPad to your computer via Wi-Fi, I strongly suggest setting up a dedicated Wi-Fi network for your home studio. Connecting music production apps wirelessly via your home Internet Wi-Fi router may result in a very poor user experience.

**Why?**

1. If your home Internet Wi-Fi router sits in a different part of your home or in a different floor, the signal has to travel the distance from the iPad to the router and back to your computer. This will cause a delay and possibly dropouts in the signal.

2. If there are multiple devices in your home that are connected to your home Internet Wi-Fi router, they are each using a portion the router's bandwidth. This will limit the available bandwidth for your music production app.

## Have Your Cake and Eat It, Too!

It is possible to have your computer connected to two networks at the same time. One network would connect to your home Internet, and the second network would be exclusively for your home studio.

To do this, you would need to purchase and set up two items:

1) An external USB Wi-Fi adapter (or dongle) such as the **USB-N13 N600** by Asus (www.asus.com).

2) A Wi-Fi router such as the **Linksys E1200** by Cisco (www.home.cisco.com).

Use your computer's existing Wi-Fi adapter for Internet connectivity, and install the external USB Wi-Fi adapter and assign it to your home studio network.

The Wi-Fi router you purchase for your studio doesn't require an Internet line from your phone or cable company. Use the router's instructions to help you create a network and call this network "Home Studio Network" or whatever you like. Make sure this router stays close to your home studio setup. Then turn on your iPad and connect it to this network instead of your Internet network when connecting to your studio applications.

**Figure 6-5:** The Asus USB-N13 N600 USB Wi-F- adapter.

**Figure 6-6:** The Linksys E1200 Wi-Fi router by Cisco.

## Key Points from Chapter 6

- Mobile devices such as the iPad can be a great addition to your home studio.
- The iPad can either be a stand-alone recording solution, a sound source for your DAW or a controller for your computer-based software.
- Set up a separate network for your home studio if you intend to use the iPad wirelessly with your computer.

# SETTING UP YOUR STUDIO

In This Chapter:

➤ Room Setup and Acoustics

➤ Working Ergonomically

➤ Home Studio Setup Examples

➤ Safeguarding Your Home Studio

## Room Setup and Acoustics

The final and arguably most important part of the listening chain is the listening environment itself. Chances are your studio will occupy space in either a bedroom, living room, dining room, attic, basement or a garage which was designed for living (or parking), and is not ideal for producing professional-sounding music.

All room spaces have their own unique acoustic idiosyncrasies based on room shape, wall and floor materials, ceiling height, and window placement (if any). You'll need to understand the reflections and frequency tendencies of your recording space, then either treat the room with sound absorption materials, or at least understand these tendencies so you can compensate for them during the recording and mixing processes.

### Optimal Desk and Speaker Placement

To begin optimizing your home studio for the best listening experience, you'll want to first place your mixing desk and reference speakers into a good position. Here are some tips to help you optimize studio desk placement to achieve the most accurate listening experience, and minimize the affect room acoustics will have on your mix.

✓ **Place your desk center between two walls and avoid corners when possible.** Bass frequencies build up in the corners and exaggerate the bass coming from your speakers. This will cause you to overcompensate the exaggerated bass by reducing the bass frequencies in your mix. The result will be bass that sounds weak on other systems compared to what you hear in your home studio.

✓ **Place your desk so your monitor speakers are at least 6-12" away from the wall.** Most monitor speakers have a rear-facing bass port (or bass reflex system). Bass ports release air from the speaker caused by woofer movement, and are designed to increase the efficiency of the speaker at lower frequencies. However, if the rear of the speaker is too close to the wall, the wall acts as a bass resonator and exaggerates the sound of the bass.

Monitor speakers with front-facing bass ports such as KRK Rokit (www.krksys.com) series speakers release air and low frequency energy out the front of the speaker away from the wall, so they don't need to adhere to the 6–12" rule. However, it's still a good practice to place speakers with front-facing bass ports at least a couple of inches away from the wall.

✓ Place your monitors at a distance apart from each other that is equal to their distance from the listening position, creating an equilateral triangle. This is covered in Chapter 3.

✓ **Face your monitors the long way into the room.** If you are in a rectangular room, it's better to face your monitors the long way into the room. Sound waves reflected off the rear wall bounce back and combine with sound waves coming directly from your monitors. The combined sound waves create what are known as standing waves. Facing your monitors the long way into your room places more distance between the listening position and the rear wall, minimizing this effect.

## Three Enemies of Good Room Acoustics

Sound waves travel from your monitor speakers then bounce back and forth between the hard parallel walls in your studio. The reflected sound continues to travel and bounce off your walls until the sound waves are eventually absorbed and die off.

Reflecting sound waves within a room create what I call the three enemies of good room acoustics:

1) Standing Waves
2) Flutter Echoes
3) Bass Buildup

**Standing waves** occur when sound waves bounce between parallel walls and combine with direct sound waves coming from your monitor speakers. Matched frequencies from the combined waves interact and cause volume peaks and dips within the room. If your listening position is within one of the peaks or dips, your mixes will be negatively influenced by the affected sound.

**Flutter echoes** are successive, repetitive reflections greater than 50 milliseconds apart, so they are perceived as different sound events. Room reverberation is the close cousin of flutter echoes with thousands of repetitive reflections happening .01 to 1 milliseconds apart. Room reverb and flutter echoes are most noticeable with sounds reflecting at higher frequencies.

**Bass buildup** is the buildup of low frequency resonance that tends to occur in the corners of a room. The human ear perceives bass frequencies below 80 Hz as omnidirectional. Also, low frequency sound waves are longer than high frequency sound waves and don't bounce around a room as quickly. For these reasons, bass frequencies tend to bounce off walls and build up in the corners, causing the sound from your monitors to appear bass-heavy and muddy.

## Three Keys to Combating Poor Room Acoustics

Standing waves, flutter echoes, room reverberations and corner bass buildup wreak havoc on your listening experience. However, these problems can be fixed with some simple treatments around the room. The object of acoustic room treatment is not to completely deaden the acoustics of the room, but you do want to control the acoustics so they don't affect your listening experience.

There are three keys to combating room acoustic problems in your home studio:

1) Isolate Sound
2) Absorb Reflections
3) Diffuse Bass

## Isolate Sound

The first step is to isolate sound sources, so they don't reflect off surfaces in your studio.

Reference monitors should be isolated (or decoupled) from your desk by placing them on dedicated speaker stands, or on sound isolating foam such as **MoPAD** Monitor Isolation Pads by Auralex (www.auralex.com).

A microphone can be isolated during recording by using a spare closet as a makeshift sound booth. Alternatively, you can use a portable isolation booth such as **Reflexion Filter Pro** portable vocal booth by SE Electronics (www.seelectronics.com).

Blankets and mattresses can be used as makeshift sound barriers to isolate instruments such as acoustic guitars and drums when recording.

## Absorb Early Reflections

The place on your walls and ceiling immediately above, left, right and behind your monitor speakers is known as the points of first reflection. Sound quickly reflects off these surfaces and is indistinguishable to your ears from the original sound source.

To treat these early reflections, sit at the listening position and have someone move a mirror along the side walls, front wall and ceiling until you see the speaker's reflection (right speaker on the right wall, left speaker on the left wall). Place an acoustic sound treatment panel or foam tiles at each of these points. The height placement of the wall treatments should be so the center height of the panel or foam is equal to the height of your speaker cones. If your studio has medium plush carpeting, the ceiling reflections are reduced and a panel here may not be necessary.

## Absorb Late Reflections

Late reflections are what we largely perceive as general ambience in a room. To control and absorb late reflections, place an acoustic panel on the rear wall and rear side walls. Like the early reflection panels, the height placement of the wall treatment should be so the center height of the panel or foam is equal to the height of your speaker cones.

## Diffuse Bass

Bass traps diffuse low frequencies, reducing bass buildup and modal ringing. which causes some notes to ring out longer than others. Most foam bass traps purchased commercially have an irregular front surface that helps to diffuse the low frequencies, while the thickness of the foam absorbs them.

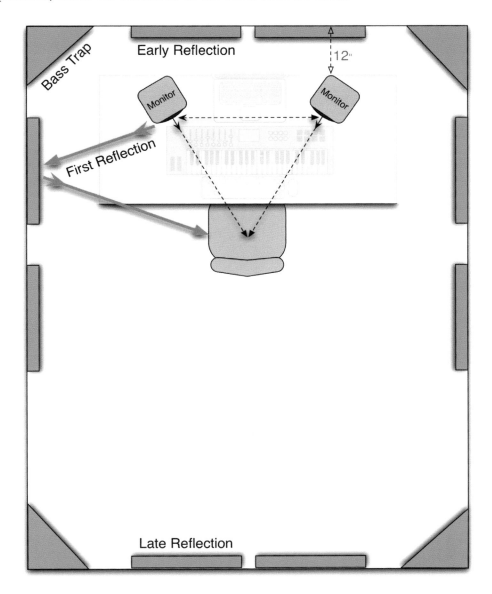

**Figure 7-1:** An example of an 8' wide by 10' long room that's acoustically balanced and treated for optimal listening. The speakers face the long way into the room and form an equilateral triangle from the listening position. Bass traps diffuse low frequency build-up in the corners, and acoustic panels absorb early and late reflections.

## Sound Treatment Panels

Sound treatment panels are made of sound-absorbing materials that help to stop reflections. There are two approaches for adding sound treatment to your space. You can purchase an acoustic foam room kit such as the **Roominator Project 2** by Aurelex, which costs about $659 (www.auralex.com). Or you can build your own acoustic panels and bass traps for $25 per 4' x 2' panel using fiberglass or rock wool insulation.

## DIY Acoustic Sound Treatment Panels

Building acoustic treatment panels yourself is not as complicated as you may think. I built eight acoustic panels for my home recording studio during a free weekend. Each panel took me about 30 to 45 minutes to build.

> ❖ For a complete description and video on how to build your own acoustic sound treatment panels visit
> http://www.homemusicproduction.com/build-acoustic-panels-for-your-home-studio/

**FAQ:** I'm recording and mixing mostly using headphones. Are the acoustics in my room still important?

Room acoustics only play a big role when you are either recording sound using a microphone, or creating a final mix of your music using monitor speakers. If you're only recording music in the box using virtual instruments, you're using headphones, and you're not using a microphone, then room acoustics will not play a role in your recordings.

## Mixing with Headphones

Mixing music using only headphones is widely frowned upon in the elite mixing community. However, there are professional studio engineers who mix using headphones. If you do this, use open-back headphones and not closed-back headphones. An example of open-back headphones used for mixing is the **AKG 702.** An example of closed-back headphones used for recording and tracking is the **AKG K 271 MK II** ([www.akg.com](www.akg.com)). Also, when mixing with headphones, it's good to mix at lower volume levels to avoid ear fatigue.

**FAQ:** Do book shelves and cabinets in rooms work as acoustic sound treatment?

Yes and no. Assuming the bookshelf is filled with books, it may diffuse or reflect sound, but not absorb it to any useful amount. Reflecting sound is what you don't want, but this will happen if the books have smooth shiny surfaces and the books are lined up creating a flat even surface.

A bookshelf with books may, however, effectively help to reduce bass frequencies in corners by deflecting the bass frequencies and not allowing them to build up there.

Cabinets or shelves without books are ineffective at controlling room acoustics. In fact, if a cabinet has glass doors or a shiny finish, it may increase sound reflections in a room.

## Sound Absorption vs. Sound proofing

When we talk about acoustic room treatments, it's important to point out the difference between sound absorption and sound proofing. What we're doing by adding acoustic panels to a room is adding dimension to a room, absorbing sound and minimizing reflections. This is different from sound proofing, which prevents sound from entering or escaping a particular space.

In sound proofing a room, studio designers build additional walls and floors containing the same sound-absorbing fiberglass or rock wool used to absorb reflections within the room. However, the sound-proofing materials are built into the walls and are designed to be a permanent part of the structure. Once sound proofing is built into the walls of a studio, diffusion and absorption panels are then built outside the walls to prevent reflections.

## Working Ergonomically

Since you'll undoubtedly spend countless hours at your production desk creating and recording music, you'll want a desk space and chair that won't have you feeling fatigued after only a few hours.

Choose a comfortable chair that allows adjustments in height and lumbar support. I like ergonomic style chairs because they tend to be made of breathable mesh material, but I've also spent countless hours in a plush leather office chair and it worked just as well. I also like a chair that either comes without the side arm rests or allows me to remove them. This way you have the option of removing them if they're in the way of working comfortably.

As for desk options, they range from full multi-tiered music production desks to simple and inexpensive one-tier or L-shaped desks from Ikea. Whichever way you go on this, make sure all of the items you'll need quick access to, such as your computer, computer keyboard, mouse and MIDI controller, are right in front of you and easily accessible. Other items can sit comfortably to the side and out of the way for a less cluttered workspace. Lastly, getting a desk with an adjustable height will be a definite plus.

Here are some tips to working ergonomically in your home studio:

✓ **Set your chair height so your feet are flat on the ground.** If your feet are dangling in the air, or if your calves and thighs are not at a 90-degree angle from each other, then your chair may be too high or too low.

✓ **Set your desk height so your forearms and wrists are horizontal when using the keyboard.** This is a good reason to get a work desk with an adjustable height such as **Galant** desks from Ikea, or the **ACD-42-56B** by Raxxes. It also goes without saying that sitting upright and avoiding slouching will help you avoid posture problems long term.

✓ **Set your computer monitor at arm's reach and eye level.**  Set your computer monitor so that the top of the monitor is at eye level.  This will prevent you from having to lower or raise your head for long periods of time to see important parts of your screen.  Also, place the monitor on your desk far back enough so it's an arm's length from your face.

✓ **Position the items you need the most so they're right in front of you.**  Being a piano player, I always prefer to have a piano keyboard right in front and slightly lower, so I can play and record comfortably.  With my previous home studio setup, I placed a 49-key MIDI keyboard on the desk directly in front of the computer monitor, then placed the computer keyboard and mouse on the desk directly in front of the MIDI keyboard.

My current studio desk has a MIDI keyboard rollout shelf.  So now my computer keyboard and mouse (actually Apple's Magic Trackpad) sit center on my desk while the MIDI keyboard rolls out when needed.

If you're a guitarist and will be recording with your guitar more often than a MIDI keyboard, place the MIDI keyboard to the side so your guitar recording is facing center.  The same is true if you're recording mainly from a groove box like NI's Maschine or Akai's MPC series groove boxes.  Keep this centered and place the MIDI keyboard off to the side.

✓ **Consider using a hardware DAW controller.**  Some DAW manufacturers produce proprietary surface controllers designed to integrate and work seamlessly with their DAWs.  Controllers such as Steinberg's CMC series controllers and Avid's Artist series controllers integrate well with Cubase and Pro Tools respectively.  They take some of the repetitive functions away from the computer mouse and provide a more tactile way of recording music.

✓ **Take a break.**  Take a 10-minute break every 50 minutes.  This is good to help get your circulation going and to clear your mind for a bit so you can come back fresh.

# Home Studio Setup Examples

Here are five examples of home recording studio setups that may help you in deciding how to configure your studio. The examples below are merely suggestions to provide you with some setup ideas.

1) Singer/songwriter who wants a simple laptop-based setup to write songs and record ideas

2) Film/video game composer recording MIDI only and needs scoring

3) Band member who needs audio recording for multiple instruments

4) DJ who needs MIDI and audio for a single microphone

5) Music producer who is recording and producing for multiple artists at home, then mixing and mastering in a commercial studio

## Singer/songwriter who wants a simple laptop-based setup to write songs and record ideas

Setup includes:

- **MacBook Pro:** Laptop with 4GB of RAM.
- **GarageBand**: Simple recording software with plenty of built-in virtual instruments and effects. Included free with the MacBook Pro.
- **M-Audio Mobile Pre:** Audio interface that provides two XLR/TR inputs so the singer can mic vocals and an acoustic instrument at the same time.
- **M-Audio BX5 D2:** Reference monitors with 5" woofer. Good for listening in smaller rooms.
- **M-Audio Axiom 49:** MIDI keyboard.
- **2-large diaphragm condenser mics**

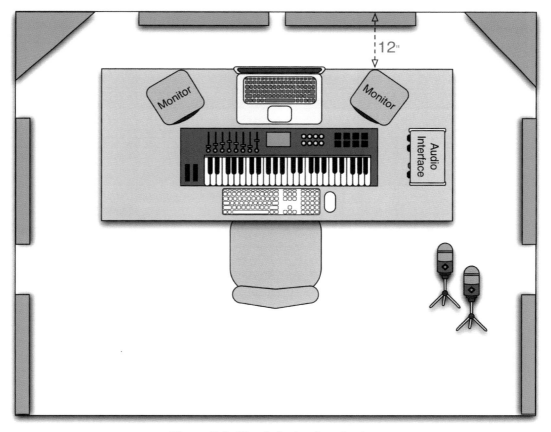

**Figure 7-2:** Simple laptop-based setup.

# Film/video game composer recording MIDI only and needs scoring

Setup includes:
- **Desktop computer/monitor:** With the number of tracks needed for scoring, a powerful PC or Mac desktop with a fast i7 processor and 16GB of RAM is required.
- **Cubase**: A full-featured DAW with powerful scoring capabilities.
- **Steinberg CI2+:** Audio interface designed to take advantage of Cubase Ai functionality. The interface is also a control surface featuring transport and other buttons for easy DAW control and navigation.
- **M-Audio BX5 D2:** Reference monitors with 5" woofer.
- **M-Audio SBX-10:** Subwoofer to hear sub bass frequencies popular in film and video game scores.
- **M-Audio Axiom 61:** MIDI keyboard.

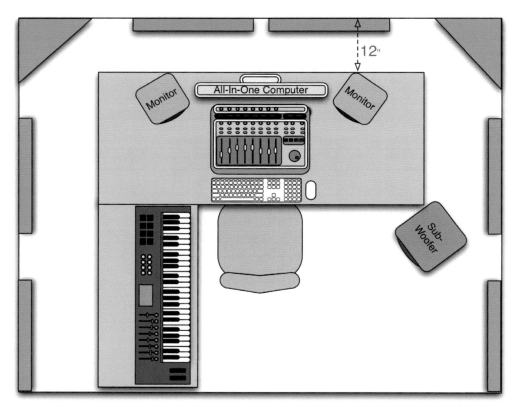

**Figure 7-3:** Computer-based setup with sub-woofer speaker and a DAW controller. For best sub-woofer placement, move your chair aside and place the sub-woofer in that spot. Play music that's been professionally mixed and mastered with good low-end frequencies. Crawl on the floor around the room until you hear the smoothest, most consistent bass sound. Mark that spot and place your sub-woofer there.

## Band member who needs audio recording for multiple instruments

Setup includes:

- **17" Laptop:** A powerful PC or Mac desktop replacement laptop with a 17" screen, so it can travel from the recording garage, to the rehearsal studio. A fast i7 processor is needed to record multiple simultaneous live tracks. A fast external hard drive is needed to store all the audio.
- **PreSonus StudioLive 16.0.2 Mixer/Interface:** A 16-channel mixer with a built-in audio interface and dynamics processing. Full integration with PreSonus Studio One DAW.
- **PreSonus Studio One Artist:** Free DAW with Studio Live 16.0.2
- **Mackie HR824 MK2:** Reference monitors with 8" woofer for mixing in a slightly larger garage or rehearsal studio environment.
- **Large diaphragm condenser and dynamic mics:** Quantity based on band and needs.

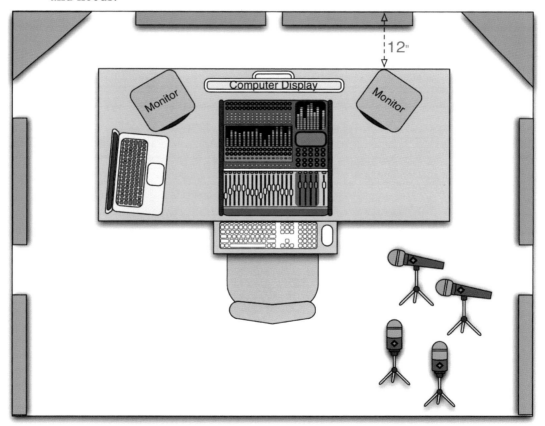

**Figure 7-4:** Laptop-based setup with 16-channel mixer with built in audio interface.

## DJ who needs MIDI and audio for a single microphone

Setup includes:
- **13" or 15" Laptop:** A PC or Mac laptop with an i7 processor that is powerful, yet small enough to add to an existing rig.
- **Ableton Live:** Pattern-based DAW focused for live performance
- **Numark Mixtrack:** Pro DJ software controller.
- **Novation Launchpad:** Ableton Live controller.
- **M-Audio Fast Track:** Simple audio interface with one XLR input for a mic and one TRS balanced input for a mono instrument.
- **KRK Rokit 5:** Reference monitors with 5" woofer.
- **KRK 10S:** Subwoofer to better hear low-end frequencies critical to music being played in a dance club.
- **M-Audio Axiom 25:** MIDI keyboard.
- **Large diaphragm condenser mic.**

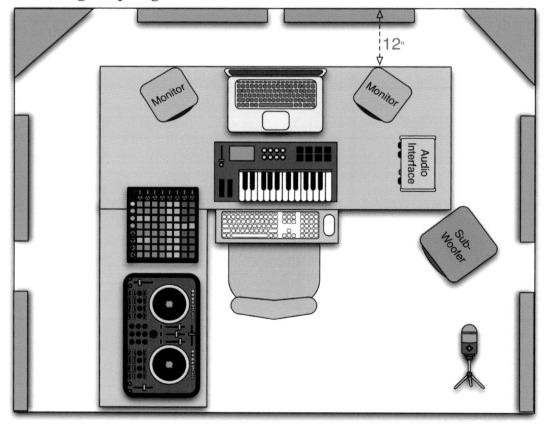

**Figure 7-5:** DJ focused setup with laptop, DJ controller and Ableton Live controller.

## Music producer who is recording and producing for multiple artists at home, then mixing and mastering at a commercial studio

Setup includes:
- **iMac 27":** iMac with i7 processor, 8GB or 16GB RAM, 27" screen.
- **Pro Tools:** Powerful DAW compatible with recording environments in most commercial studios.
- **Avid Mbox Pro:** Audio interface with 8 inputs to record lead and backup vocals simultaneously. Comes bundled with Pro Tools.
- **KRK Rokit 5:** Reference monitors with 5" woofer since music is being mixed at a commercial studio
- **M-Audio Axiom 49:** MIDI keyboard.
- **Native Instruments Maschine:** Groove production drum machine.
- **Large diaphragm condenser mics.** For lead and backup vocals.

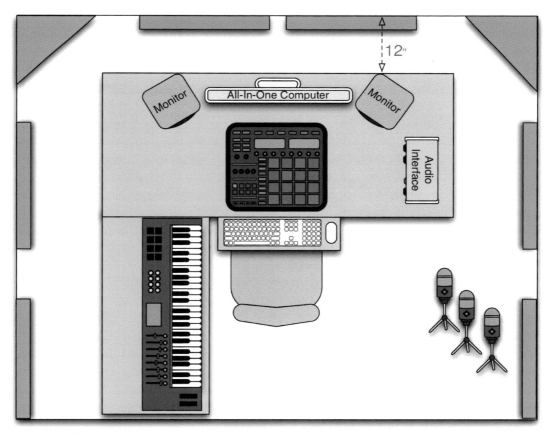

Figure 7-6: Computer-based setup with groove focused production.

# Safeguarding Your Home Studio

Once you've made the investment in your new home recording studio, it's important to take steps to safeguard your hardware, software and creative works. After all, the investment you make into your music production hardware and software is costly, but the gems you create with your production setup are priceless.

Here are five steps you can take to safeguard your home studio:

1) Back-up your hard drives
2) Protect software product licenses
3) Store CD/DVD software in a fire-safe chest
4) Use an uninterrupted power source (UPS)
5) Get home or renters insurance

## Back-up your hard drives

This goes without saying and yet I'm amazed how often this essential step is overlooked. PCs with Windows 7 operating system come with "Backup and Restore" pre-installed, so you can back up all hard drive volumes on your computer. Mac OS X comes pre-installed with "Time Machine." Also hard drive manufacturers such as Seagate and Western Digital often have a backup utility pre-installed on their hard drives.

For my home studio computer, I use Time Machine to back up my entire system to a 2 Terabyte hard drive. I also use a cloud storage service to specifically back up my DAW project files, finished recordings and downloaded software. Only this level of redundancy allows me to rest peacefully at night.

## Protect software product licenses

In today's software-driven recording environment, we pay hundreds of dollars for downloaded software including DAWs, synth plug-ins and effect bundles. With these purchases, the product license is what you're paying for. If you change computers and need to re-install the software, you'll need to have the product key code saved somewhere. Save the original emails or keep the actual product code information safe somewhere and not on your local computer. I save software license codes in the original email, and I have one master file that I keep with all license codes copied to it. This is also backed-up in cloud storage.

Some software developers use product license dongles such as iLok (www.iLok.com), which has both advantages and disadvantages. An advantage (specific to iLok) is that it can hold several product licenses on one dongle to avoid having three or four dongles using up precious USB slots. One bad point is that if your gear is stolen or melted in a fire, your license dongle isn't much good. iLok has a disaster recovery program called "Zero Downtime" which will replace the iLok licenses if they're ever lost or destroyed, and the service is well worth the $30 annual cost per iLok.

### Store CD/DVD software in a fire-safe chest

Although much music production software is available via download, many DAWs and virtual instruments containing multi-gigabytes of data are only available on CDs or DVDs. Instead of storing your new virtual drum sampler software with the nice colorful box in the closet, recycle the box and get a fire-safe chest to store the discs in. Fire- and water-safe chests such as ones made by Sentry (www.sentrysafe.com) can provide your CDs, DVDs and USB drives up to one hour of fire protection up to 1,700 degrees Fahrenheit. They're also waterproof to protect against floods. For less than $70, you can pick one up at Walmart, Target or Costco, and it's well worth it.

### Use an uninterrupted power source (UPS)

Power outages are a regular occurrence in my town, so a UPS is indispensable. But even if you live in an area with very few power outages, just remember it only takes one outage or spike in the grid to turn any component within your recording studio into a highly priced toaster. A UPS (which is a battery backup source) that is sufficient for a home recording studio will cost about $170, but is substantially less than replacing a fried computer or MIDI synthesizer workstation. A UPS such as ones made by APC (www.apc.com) or CyberPower (www.cyberpowersystems.com) can keep your setup safe and running on battery power for several minutes. This provides you enough time to power down safely or continue recording for several minutes after the power has gone out.

### Get home or renters insurance

I know this is an expensive one, but it ranks high in importance. Get home owners or renters insurance in an amount that will cover the cost of your studio in the event of theft, fire or flood. Renters insurance is pretty clear in that you get it specifically to cover the items inside your home. Homeowners insurance can be less clear as you may have different levels of insurance that cover exterior property damage but may not cover your studio inside. While this will set you back a few hundred dollars a year, the alternative is purchasing your entire studio again from scratch at a time when you may not have all the ability to do so.

## Key Points from Chapter 7
- Position your desk and speakers to optimize your listening experience.
- Even the most expensive studio monitors can sound poorly in an acoustically untreated room, so make this a priority.
- Get a desk and chair that adjusts to keep your calves and thighs at a 90-degree angle, and your forearms and hands horizontal when using your keyboard.
- Use a UPS to protect your gear from power spikes and outages.
- Backup, backup, backup!

# FINAL THOUGHTS

Hopefully you are now on your way to building an ergonomic and great-sounding recording studio. Start out with the basics needed to record music, learn these tools first, and then expand your palette of tools as needed.

Let's recap some key points discussed in this book:

- Make sure you understand your computer needs before purchasing your computer laptop or desktop. Also, everything will run smoother with more RAM. Even if you're getting the minimum RAM at the time of purchase, ensure your computer will upgrade to a minimum of 8GB of RAM.

- Choose a DAW that flows with your creative style and workflow. Consider your needs before making the leap. Learn your DAW inside and out.

- Don't get too wrapped up in acquiring virtual instruments and effects. The instruments and especially the effects that come with complete DAW packages will get the job done. Watch out for marketing jargon like "this plug-in will warm up your tracks." A similar sound can be achieved using EQ.

- If you're using monitor speakers to play or mix music, then the acoustics in your studio are just as important to your listening experience as the speakers. By fixing a few common acoustic problems in your studio, your monitors will sound better.

- Minimize noise in your studio by using balanced cables with the shortest length possible. Use Velcro or other cable ties to keep cable runs neat.

- Protect your investment by using a UPS and, most importantly, by backing up your work and software.

Getting your studio set up is only the first step to achieving great recordings. Once your studio is set up, sounds good, is working the way you need it to, and is comfortable and ergonomic, the next step is to learn the techniques needed to optimize your recordings and mixes.

Mixing and mastering music is one part science, one part craft and one part art form. Keep in mind that recording engineers spend years honing this craft just as musicians spend years learning to play instruments. Don't be discouraged if your initial mixes don't sound as good as your favorite commercial recordings.

Open up your favorite commercially available music in your DAW and study its production and mix as it plays through your monitor speakers –keeping in mind that this music has also been professionally mastered. Study the frequencies of that music using a spectrum analyzer. When mixing your own music, use your ears, but also check the frequency balance in a spectrum analyzer and work your mix until it has a similar balance to your professionally mixed reference music.

Please register at www.HomeMusicProduction.com to receive notifications on book updates, and to receive the latest information, product reviews and tips on producing music in your new home recording studio.

I appreciate your feedback on this book; please send me your comments through our website at www.HomeMusicProduction.com/Getting-Started

You can also connect with me online:

Facebook: www.facebook.com/HomeMusicProduction
YouTube: www.youtube.com/user/searlstudio
Twitter: www.twitter.com/searlstudio

Happy music creating!